BE BLESSED, DEAR REBECCA, BE BLESSED.

Gena

TAKE TWO

WHEN YOU DON'T GET IT RIGHT THE FIRST TIME

GENA MCMYNE

WESTBOW
PRESS®
A DIVISION OF THOMAS NELSON
& ZONDERVAN

WestBow Press books may be ordered through booksellers or by contacting:

WestBow Press
A Division of Thomas Nelson & Zondervan
1663 Liberty Drive
Bloomington, IN 47403
www.westbowpress.com
1 (866) 928-1240

ISBN: 978-1-9736-8625-5 (sc)
ISBN: 978-1-9736-8624-8 (hc)
ISBN: 978-1-9736-8626-2 (e)

Library of Congress Control Number: 2020903635

Print information available on the last page.

WestBow Press rev. date: 03/11/2020

To all those who need to be reminded that our God is a God of second chances. May these words give you hope and help you begin to live in victory, free of the guilt and shame of your past mistakes. My heartfelt prayers are with you.

Contents

Foreword

I can still remember the cold February night that Gena and I met for the first time. The room was dimly lit, and there were many people around us. While sitting at the table with our friends, my words were few. To make a long story short, near the end of the night, we had our first dance together.

As we were leaving the establishment, we hugged at the bottom of the stairs, and yes, she gave me her real phone number. The hug was beyond a normal first-time meeting hug. We both knew at that exact moment there was more to come.

The next day, I called her, and we had our first real date—a walk in a nearby state park that gave us a chance to begin to get to know each other. As we walked together, my mind kept going back to the thought, *How can this beautiful girl be interested in me?* A year later, we were married and started our life's journey together as a couple.

Gena came to faith in Christ long before me. After she returned home from the spiritual weekend where she was saved, I noticed an instant transformation in her and was not sure how to handle the change. She was more caring, more giving, more loving. Everything was new. I had never experienced someone changing this dramatically. She was so full of the Spirit of the Lord that when she walked into a room, hurting women were drawn to her.

For the next fourteen years, I continued on my unsaved journey, not knowing that my wife and several of her Bible study friends were praying for my salvation. Yes, I said fourteen years! Talk about fervent prayer! Then there was that day in August 1995 that I gave my life to the Lord, and my life was changed forever!

Since then, Gena was called into the ministry as a pastor, a spiritual director on retreat weekends, a musician, an author, and a counselor. She has also worked with children with emotional issues in the local school district. Full of compassion, full of wisdom, and full of understanding, she ministered to these beautiful young people.

Also, I can't count the number of times that her phone rings each day with someone in need of prayer or healing. She ministers to each one with the love of Jesus.

When there are incidents where people need special attention from her, I stand back in awe and watch our wonderful Lord work through His willing vessel. Their hurts become her hurts.

One day, Gena came to me with an idea for a

prayer room—a place where she could study, pray, and maybe even write a book without any interruptions. So we selected an empty bedroom in our home, and the construction began.

The day I put the finishing touches on the prayer room, I wasn't fully aware of what would actually happen in this space. There was no desk. There were empty bookshelves, new lights, and new carpeting, but it was still an empty room. But then I remembered that underneath the new carpeting were scriptures Gena had written on the plywood subfloor before the carpet was installed. So whatever activity was going to take place in this room was going to be fruitful because she was standing on the Word of God, the truth.

Next, the bookshelves were filled to capacity, and a desk was placed against the wall. The place became her own as she thoughtfully decorated the room with crosses, pictures, and various knickknacks that would inspire her.

The finishing touch was a beautiful hand-made altar crafted for her in love by our youngest son, Chris, that would become the focal point of this prayer sanctuary. Most every morning at five thirty, for an average of two hours plus, I know my spirit-filled wife is in this sanctuary on her knees at the altar in prayer, interceding, or reading the Word of God, or just waiting for Him to speak to her. It is very evident that she has a strong relationship with the Lord because

I see the fruit of the Spirit in all that Gena lays her hands on.

Also, my heart melts when I hear my wife sweetly say, "God is patiently waiting for me every morning in my prayer room."

I would like to thank the Lord for this beautiful, spirit-filled, Christian woman he has placed in my life. We have shared so many experiences together in the last forty-three years, prayed together, cried many tears together, rejoiced together, and been blessed so many times and in so many ways, especially with the family and friends He has given to us to love.

I continue to watch the transformation of the beautiful girl I met forty-three years ago, into the most amazing, beautiful woman I have ever known.

Gena is the most precious earthly treasure that the Lord has given to me to love, honor, and cherish for all the days of my life.

This book that you are about to read is the result of many hours of prayer, many life experiences, and some heartache when revisiting those experiences. I believe that Gena's desire to write this book comes from her extraordinary relationship with her Savior and her willingness to share her life experiences with others who are hurting, stuck in the guilt and shame of their past mistakes.

As you read this incredible book, be mindful that these words that you see printed on each page have been given to Gena by the Holy Spirit of Almighty God, for the purpose of transforming your life forever.

May all the praise and honor and glory be to God, for the great things He has done!

—Gary McMyne

Acknowledgments

First and foremost, I thank God the Father, for never giving up on me and always giving me a second chance; Jesus, His son, for the gift of my salvation; and the Holy Spirit, for guiding me every step of the way. Oh, how I love You.

This book would never have been written had it not been for the love and encouragement of one man—my dear husband, Gary. You have been my confidant and my sounding board. Your constant faith in me gave me the courage to believe in myself and push through the hard times. Thank you from the bottom of my heart for helping make my dream come true. May each passing year find us more in love.

To my three amazing sons, Mike, Scott, and Chris: it is in your honor this book is written. These words are your legacy. Learn from them, my boys. Never forget how much you are loved.

To my beautiful daughters-in-love, Jen and Victoria: you are strong, confident, loving women. I've learned so much in this process through your example. You are the daughters of my heart.

To my delightful grandchildren, Cayden, Kayleigh,

Anthony, Elijah, and Caroline: you are my joy. Your smiles, hugs, and unconditional love make my heart sing. I love you more than words can say.

To my brother, Gary: you have always seen the good in me. Throughout the years, your encouraging words have challenged me to look past my self-doubts and soar. It is because of you that this book reached completion. How blessed I am to have you not only as a brother but one of my best friends.

To my beloved aunt Gena: you have filled so many roles in my life—mother, friend, aunt, and sister. You stood by me through all the laughter and all the tears, through all the ups and downs of life. Your faith in me is what has made this book possible. I couldn't have done it without you. I love you so.

To my editor and dear friend, Carol: words cannot express the depth of my gratitude for the countless hours you spent poring over chapter after chapter. Your honesty was always tempered with a measure of love and grace. I am a better writer and a better person because of you.

To my dear friends Rhonda, Carla, Linda, Anne Marie, Lori, Cindy Lu, Colleen, Debbie, Dee Dee, Robin, Vicki, Tristyn, Pattii, Mary Lou, Ally, Betsy, Louise, Shirley, Jan and so many more: for all the times you listened, prayed, encouraged, and supported me, I thank you from the bottom of my heart.

To WestBow Press: you have accomplished what I

thought was impossible. You've taken this frightened, technologically allergic woman and turned her into a confident, savvy writer. Thank you to my incredible team for treating me with such kindness and helping me work through all the insecurities. I am so very grateful.

Introduction

Look in the mirror … That's your competition.

—Eric Thomas

So many of us have a distorted view of ourselves. We look in the mirror and see every flaw that time and circumstances have produced. Instead of remembering the moments when we followed God's lead or spoke the right words at the perfect time, we tend to dwell on the memory of those instances when we came up short. We may even know we've been forgiven by God, but somewhere deep in our souls, we bear the anguish and regret no one sees. We are unable to move forward because we simply can't get past our mistakes. In short, we're stuck. News flash: we're not perfect, nor are we expected to be.

Welcome to *Take Two: When You Don't Get It Right the First Time*. Do you find yourself tired of letting the guilt and shame of your past mistakes control you? Then this book is for you. You've listened to the wrong voices for far too long and desperately want to change that. You long to be all God's calling you to be, but your feelings of unworthiness are holding you captive. My friend, you have come to the right place.

In the book of Galatians, the great apostle Paul speaks of the kind of fruit the Holy Spirit produces in our lives once we accept Jesus as Lord and Savior. We should be displaying love, joy, peace, patience, kindness, goodness, faithfulness, gentleness, and self-control. Many of us have been taught, however, that if every one of these attributes is not in perfect alignment, then something is wrong with us. Our relationship with God can't be what it's supposed to be, and our spiritual life is somehow lacking. That kind of thinking has left many a believer feeling hopeless, as though they will never be able to measure up. I am here to tell you that our God is a God of second chances. Praise His name!

I want you to know that it has taken me years to discover the secrets of living a victorious life despite my imperfections, my mistakes, and the words that were spoken over me. My prayer as you journey through the pages of this book is that you will realize you're not alone. May you be inspired by the personal stories from my own life, learn from my mistakes, and feel the presence and the power of the Holy Spirit throughout these writings. It truly is my heart's desire that you will find this book to be a breath of fresh air and one that leads you on a path to liking the image you see in the mirror—the unique, unrepeatable miracle God created you to be.

Included at the end of each chapter is a "Time to Reflect" section. I would encourage you to take your time with every piece, be honest with yourself, and allow the Holy Spirit to speak life into your hurting soul.

I am so thankful you chose this book as part of your healing journey. Know that I will be praying for you as you travel this road toward a brand-new life in Him. Be blessed, dear one, be blessed.

But the fruit of the Spirit is love, joy, peace, patience, kindness, goodness, faithfulness, gentleness, self-control ...

—Galatians 5:22–23 NASB

Love

God teaches us love by putting some
unlovely people around us
—Rick Warren

What the world needs now is love, sweet love
It's the only thing that there's just too little of
What the world needs now is love, sweet love
No not just for some but for everyone
—lyrics by Hal David

When I close my eyes, I can still hear Jackie DeShannon
singing those beautiful words. The year was 1965. The
United States was enmeshed in the war in Vietnam.
Though a large majority of the American population
supported the administration, a small but outspoken
group of more liberal young people began to express
their opposition. As a result, what began as peaceful

protests quickly escalated, and the antiwar movement kicked into high gear. We were suddenly a country divided. Much to the surprise of its songwriters, "What the World Needs Now Is Love" won the hearts of people on both sides of that political fence.

Why? Because no truer words had ever been spoken. The world needed love. It wasn't the first time, and it would certainly not be the last. Let's face it, folks. We all need love, don't we? Receiving it is one thing. Knowing how to give it is quite another. Unfortunately, it sometimes takes a catastrophe or a life-changing event to make us realize how very important love is—not just to us but to God.

Have you ever wondered why love is listed as the very first attribute of what the Bible refers to as the fruit of the Spirit? The answer is simple. This trait enables us to develop the other characteristics. Jesus was very clear on that point when He said, "You must love the LORD your God with all your heart, all your soul, and all your mind.' This is the first and greatest commandment. A second is equally important: 'Love your neighbor as yourself'" (Matthew 22:37–40 NLT).

A dear friend of mine has a perpetual smile on her face. Some have questioned her authenticity, even referring to her as a phony. Nothing could be further from the truth. She is as genuine as they come. You see, this sweet woman has never known anything but love. That's exactly how she describes her life, and that fact has colored everything in her world.

Not everyone can make such a claim, though. As a matter of fact, I would say that a very small number of people have felt that kind of love as children. I know I didn't—at least not from the woman who gave me life. I often wonder how different my world might have been if I had known my mother loved me. Yet God, in His infinite wisdom, knew exactly what it would take to form me into the loving, giving, strong, compassionate person He created me to be. What did He do? He placed me in the care of a mom who was on her own at the tender age of fourteen, through no fault of her own. She spent her teen years working for strangers for room and board, feeling alone and unloved. By the time I came along, many years later, she had no idea how to love a little girl. But then, how could she? Perhaps she felt it her responsibility to make sure I was tough enough to withstand whatever life threw at me. I just never once took any of that into consideration until God began a work in me.

I had what some might call an *interesting* start to life. I am the youngest of three, with two older brothers gracing the planet before me. My mother was perfectly happy with her two darling boys and made it very clear to anyone who would listen that she and my father had expanded their little family as much as they were going to. Imagine her surprise when she discovered she was pregnant with me. It was not exactly a Hallmark moment. She endured a very difficult pregnancy and an even more difficult birth, which nearly took both our lives. The experience didn't exactly endear me to my mother's heart.

Then there were my brothers. Gary, the younger of the two, had what he thought was a very simple solution to the problem. He peered into the cradle and, with all the finesse of a six-year-old, asked ever so politely, "She's nice, but can't we trade her for Aunt Dorothy's dog?" In other words, I wasn't exactly a welcome addition.

But to my father, I was every inch the princess, Daddy's little girl. He worked many long hours to support not just our family but my mother's relatives, who all lived with us at one time or another. Though his job kept him away from us much of the time, he never missed a school concert or even a softball game. He was there for every event in my life, from kindergarten graduation to my induction into the National Honor Society. He was the one I ran to when I was frightened or hurt or just couldn't manage on my own. In my eyes, he was the greatest man on earth.

Life was not quite as sweet with my mother, however. I don't remember her ever holding me. In my mind, it was evident as far back as memory serves that she just didn't like me or even want me.

Not surprisingly, I grew to be a troubled teenager.

Though I wasn't *in* trouble, I was so very unhappy and always searching for that one thing that would make me good enough, smart enough, pretty enough, or thin enough. Unfortunately, I couldn't find it anywhere. On the outside, I appeared to be a girl who had the world by the tail—National Honor Society student, friends from all walks of life, a fairly accomplished musician, involved in a plethora of clubs and activities, and always wearing a smile that said, "I'm fine." Yet there was a deep hurt inside, the kind no one sees.

It was 1972, and the wildly popular TV show *The Waltons* had become a regular part of our Thursday-night routine. The show was set in a small town in the hills of Virginia during the 1930s and '40s and based on the life of Earl Hamner, the story's creator. Each episode was told through the eyes of its main character, John-Boy—an aspiring young author and journalist. Over its ten-year run, I came to adore Grandma, Grandpa, Mama, Daddy, and all seven of the children that made up this amazing family. But it was John-Boy who had my full attention each week. You see, in my heart of hearts, in that place I didn't allow anyone to see, I longed to be an author like him, weaving beautiful stories with just the right combination of fact and fiction. He had such a command of the language that even his journal entries spoke to me.

Though I had excelled in creative writing, I was desperately afraid of not measuring up to my mother's standards. In order to put my thoughts on paper at home, I needed to keep them a secret. Late at night, while everyone was fast asleep, I would write to my heart's content and hide my journal in a place I thought was safe—under my mattress. Regrettably, its innocent beginnings turned sour as my writing became more and more fictional with each raging teenage hormone.

It wasn't long before insecurity turned to outright fear. I worried with every stroke of the pen that someone might read my words and think I really was the out-of-control girl my journal entries spoke of. Anxiety wasn't enough to stop me, though. Every negative comment my mother made to or about me did nothing but add fuel to the fire and more and more passion to my writing.

Looking back, I should have listened to that still, small voice whispering my name in the beginning, telling me to stop. At the time, it seemed that my guilty conscience was speaking. It never once occurred to me that it was the voice of God Himself, trying to spare me from what would lie ahead if I didn't turn back.

The worst-case scenario played over and over in my head. My mother would discover my journal, read it, and tear me apart with nothing more than a look of disgust. Oh, if it had only been that simple. I never could have anticipated the horror of what was to come.

I arrived home from school one day to find Mom sitting at the dining room table, journal in hand. I could barely breathe. My worst nightmare had come true. By the time she discovered my writings, about 98 percent of them were fabrications. Try as I might, however, there was no convincing her of that. In her mind, it was confirmation that I would never amount to anything. At least that's the way I interpreted her words.

As if I wasn't humiliated enough, she refused to return the journal. No amount of begging, pleading, or tears would change her mind. She had all the leverage she needed to threaten me with my own words, believing the girl on those pages was the real me. In her distorted way of thinking, everyone in my world who thought well of me should know who I really was. I knew what she was capable of and had no doubt that one day she might make good on her promise to ruin me.

And so I blamed my mother for everything "bad" about me—everything I was, everything I wasn't, everything I did, everything I became—and I hated her for it.

By the middle of my senior year, I came to the brilliant deduction that attending college far from home was the answer. Freed from her critical spirit, I would finally be able to find out who I really was.

College life was a mixture of all I had hoped for and everything I never wanted. Vulnerable and insecure, with newfound freedom, it was easy for me to slide right into the party scene. Drinking like a fish and experimenting with drugs became the norm. Considering the number of times I drove my car in a drunken stupor, it's only by the grace of God that I'm even alive. Looking in the mirror one day, I realized the face staring back at me was someone I didn't even know, nor did I like her. In my warped way of thinking, it was my mother's fault. If she had loved me, none of this would have happened.

While still in college, I met the man I would eventually marry and thought we would live happily ever after, that I was finally pretty enough, smart enough, and thin enough. Marrying him would surely make my mother proud to call me her daughter. Instead, she said he deserved better. Until that moment, I'd been holding onto a shred of hope that one day she would start to see me as something besides a lost cause. But her cruel words sank deep into my soul. I gave up believing anything would ever change her opinion of me, and my hatred toward her grew to astronomical proportions.

When my father died, I was thirty-eight years old and absolutely devastated. By then, I had come to faith in Jesus Christ (more about that in the next chapter). Knowing the responsibility of caring for my ailing mother was going to fall on me, I questioned God through my tears. "Why is she the parent you left me with? Why, God? Why? I can't do this. How can you expect me to?"

I knew the Bible said to honor your mother and father, but I had no idea how to do that. Thus began my quest to understand. What I discovered was the Greek word for honor means "to revere, prize, and value." How was I supposed to do that? How could I be expected to revere this woman after the way she had treated me my whole life?

The words of the fifth commandment kept ringing in my ears, though. "Honor your father and mother. Then you will live a long, full life in the land the Lord your God is giving you" (Exodus 20:12 NLT). I suddenly realized that it's the only commandment with a promise. If I didn't act according to God's instructions, He wouldn't bless me fully. That stark realization was a smack in the face. I was instantly aware of my wrong thinking and knew what needed to be done.

For seven long years, I tried to make myself honor her, doing everything I could to meet her needs. Nevertheless, the revelation I had received from the Lord could not seem to make that short trip from my head to my heart. I begged God to forgive me and to help me learn to honor and respect my mother, the woman who had given me life. While lying on the floor, curled up in a ball, sobbing gut-wrenching tears, pictures of Mom came to the forefront of my memory—images I had long forgotten. Caring for me when I was sick, creating wardrobes for my vast array of Barbie dolls, preparing special birthday dinners, and so on. That side of her, that loving, caring Mommy from my childhood had been hidden from my view for years. Her words throughout my life had damaged me to the point where I could see nothing good in her. I've heard it said that it takes at least five positive comments to overcome one negative remark. There simply had not been enough affirmations to heal those wounds. But it was in those Godsent moments on the floor that a change began in my heart. The weight of my bitterness and unforgiveness lifted, and an unexplainable urgency for her to know Jesus came over me. And for the first time, I prayed for her salvation.

I had been attending a Bible study at the home of a dear friend. Our teacher and his wife were scheduled to leave for Israel the next week. The Holy Spirit had been nudging me to give my mother's name to those two dear folks to place in one of the cracks in the Western Wall. Truth be told, I felt more than a little bit foolish asking my friends to do this. After all, there's no magic there. All the hype over that place was really nothing more than a marketing gimmick to lure unsuspecting tourists to that site. At least that's what I told myself. However, all my resistance did nothing to dissuade the Holy Spirit. Deep in my soul, I knew what needed to be done and finally gave in.

Swallowing my apprehensions, I approached this godly couple, hoping not to appear foolish. Much to my surprise, they were absolutely thrilled to do me this favor. An act of obedience. That's all it was. When our friends left for Israel, my mother was in the hospital, fighting for her life. I prayed every day that God would reach her before it was too late. Yet the more I tried to convince her of her need for a savior, the harder she dug in her heels. As painfully difficult as it was to accept, I knew she would never listen to me. God would have to send someone else. Part of me wanted to give up altogether. It would have been so much easier not to care. After all, she was sealing her own fate. But God is so good! He never let me give in to that temptation. Every time those feelings of hopelessness started to overtake me, the familiar words in John 3:16 would grace my thoughts: "For God so loved the world that He gave His one and only son, that whoever believes in Him shall not perish, but have eternal life" (John 3:16 NLT). My job wasn't over. It was simply changing. My assignment was to be on my knees in prayer.

For the next two weeks, every time my mother came to mind, I prayed for the right person, God's choice, to lead her to a saving knowledge of Him. For the most part, I had forgotten about her name being placed in the cracks of the Western Wall.

The days slipped by. There was little improvement

in Mom's condition. How was God going to answer my prayer? Who would He send? I pictured in my mind a sweet, caring nurse in whom my mother had come to trust. She would enter the room one evening after visiting hours, saying that God had sent her. Mom's heart would be strangely warmed, and she would listen with rapt attention, hanging on every word. Then, without fanfare or tears, she would simply bow her head, confess her sins, admit her need for a savior, and ask Jesus to be the Lord of her life. That seemed perfectly natural to me. Yet God had other plans.

It had become my practice to plan my hospital visits around the early-morning hours. On one particular day, however, life got crazy, and I couldn't get there until evening. Little did I know that was all a part of God's plan. For on that day, the least likely person, a friend I had all but lost touch with, became the answer to my prayer. She had heard about Mom and felt inspired to visit. With Bible in hand, she entered the hospital room with a twinge of apprehension, having experienced my mother's stubbornness on more than one occasion. Nevertheless, she was on an assignment from God, and nothing was going to stop her.

She greeted Mom with a smile, a hug, and the appropriate amount of small talk. After a few minutes had passed, she opened her Bible, laid out the plan of salvation, and calmly invited this hard-hearted woman to receive Jesus. Imagine her surprise when my mother said yes!

Though Mom kept the most important decision of her life to herself, there was an instant change in her attitude. There was only one explanation. The Lord had answered my prayer. A quick call to my friend confirmed my hopes, and I fell to my knees and thanked God for His faithfulness.

Little did I know, the story was far from over. Thousands of miles away, on the other side of the world, a miracle was taking place. At the exact time Mom was giving her heart to the Lord in a hospital bed in Johnson City, New York, our dear friends were praying fervently for her as they pressed that little piece of paper in one of the cracks in the Western Wall in Jerusalem. God had truly answered my prayer in a most unexpected way.

I watched her decline rapidly, and we knew the end was very near. She hadn't been able to speak to us in quite some time. How could our relationship ever be healed? Though it seemed impossible, I continued to pray. One night, I was awakened from a sound sleep, sat straight up in bed, and said to my husband, "I have to go to the hospital!" Sensing my urgency, he encouraged me to go—quickly. I wondered if Mom had passed. A sense of dread consumed me.

All was quiet in the sparkling clean lobby of the hospital—as would be expected at three o'clock in the morning. For once, the elevator wasn't even jammed with people—a welcome sight—though it did seem to be operating at a snail's pace. I stepped into the vacant elevator and pressed the button for the third floor.

One ... two ... three ... Come on, door, open already!

Finally arriving at the third floor, I raced down the hallway, my squeaky sneakers echoing with every step. Much to my surprise, a nurse was coming out of Mom's room. I braced myself for the worst. One look at me, though, and her mouth dropped open, a look of shock crossing her face. "I can't believe you're here! Your mother is awake and lucid. Go see her."

What? How could this be?

So many questions flooded my mind. Yet time was of the essence. I tiptoed into her room, not knowing what to expect. There was Mom, sitting up in bed, smiling and reaching for my hand. She actually reached for my hand! Walking to the side of her bed, I took her hand in mine. For the next five hours, I prayed with her, sang every hymn I knew, asked her forgiveness, and even told her I loved her ... and for the first time in my life, I meant it. With tears rolling down her face, she looked at me with such love and squeezed my hand. I knew it was her way of saying she loved me too.

Early in the morning, my cousins, knowing the gravity of my mother's physical condition, stopped by for a visit. The moment they walked in the room, it was like a curtain closed. Mom went right back to the nonresponsive state she was in before I had arrived. What a gift God had given us! He heard my prayer and provided a way for Mom and me to heal our broken relationship, forgiving me for dishonoring her in the process. In those moments, I realized the Lord had taught me how to love by placing me in the care of someone I once thought of as unlovely. How great is our God!

Time to Reflect

At this moment, I encourage you to think back to your own upbringing. For some of you, this will be a delightful experience accompanied with a mixture of smiles and tears as you recall tender moments with your parents, siblings, and extended family. For others, this little trip back in time may not be as pleasant, with painful memories you'd rather not revisit. The rest of you will find this exercise in introspection to be an interesting mix of the good, the bad, and the ugly. In any case, take this time to pause and reflect on your beginnings. Be honest with yourself, my friend. God would like nothing more than to love you to wholeness.

- Who were you then?
- Has your past shaped who you are today? How?
- Do you think it has affected your own love walk? How?
- Is there a broken relationship waiting to be restored?

Create in me a clean heart, O God.
Renew a loyal spirit within me.
—Psalm 51:10 NLT

O God, I am so very thankful for the upbringing I had. Through my family, I learned appropriate, Godly love. Through You, I learned to love others. But I'm ashamed to say I don't always get it right. Please forgive me for the times I've not represented You well to those around me. Thank You for being "a God of forgiveness, gracious and merciful, slow to become angry, and rich in unfailing love" (Nehemiah 9:17 NLT). Help me to be more like You.

Father God, the painful memories of my childhood have haunted me far too long. I've listened to the wrong voices and believed the lies of the enemy as a result. I long to be made whole. Help me, Lord, to see myself as You see me: a unique, unrepeatable miracle, crafted by Your loving hand. According to Your Word, I ask You to restore everything the enemy has stolen. Thank You, Lord, for being with me, for taking great delight in me, and for calming me with Your love (Zeph. 3:17 NLT). Help me to see myself as You see me.

Lord God, I am a mixed bag of emotions—grateful for the ways You poured out Your love on me as a child but somehow still stuck in the hurtful memories of my past. I am so thankful that You are exactly who You say You are—my protector, my provider, my comforter, my healer. You are "slow to anger and filled with unfailing love and faithfulness" (Ex. 34:6 NLT). Even in those dark corners of my past when I couldn't see or feel You, You were always near me. Thank You, Lord, for Your faithfulness. Help me to focus on Your goodness.

Joy

The Bible teaches that true joy is formed in
the midst of the difficult seasons of life.

—Francis Chan

Wouldn't it be wonderful if our entry into life here on
planet Earth included a money-back guarantee? What
if we were given the opportunity to trade this life back
in if there wasn't enough joy in the journey to suit us?
But it's not quite that easy, is it?

The Christian life is a most interesting adventure.
Sometimes the path ahead of us is smooth and easy.
Aren't those times wonderful? It makes us feel as
though all is right with the world. At other times, the
road is full of twists, turns, and potholes. We no sooner
get our bearings when yet another hazard appears
unexpectedly, catching us off guard. The obstacles
can be overwhelming, threatening to steal our joy.

Let's face it. We might have the assurance that our heavenly Father has designed this road to prepare us for the next leg of our journey with Him. Having that knowledge doesn't always make it easier though, does it? Joy does not magically present itself simply because we have no real problems at the moment.

If anyone knew the secret to having joy in the journey, it was the apostle Paul. Several of his letters to the churches were written while he was under house arrest. As a matter of fact, one of the central themes in the book of Philippians is joy. How about that? He was a prisoner and still rejoicing.

Please hear me, though. There are circumstances in life that knock us flat. There's no doubt about that. For the most part, however, we do the best we can with what we know at the time. Never forget you are a work in progress. Maya Angelou once said, "Do the best you can until you know better. Then when you know better, do better." Dear friends, that is all God expects. I must admit it took a long, hard, winding road for me to come to a full understanding of that.

My parents used to tell me that marriage is a two-way street—that it's all about giving and taking, mostly giving. But in the distorted picture in my mind where Daddy was the knight in shining armor and Mom was the wicked witch, I only saw my mother on the receiving end. I paid little to no attention to the fact that she really did perform many good deeds. I just didn't see myself as being a recipient.

I thought my parents' relationship was *the* example of what marriage was meant to look like, where Mom made the rules and Dad happily went along with whatever she said without question. I suppose to the outside world he was considered henpecked. Yet I saw him as perfect—perfect husband, perfect father, perfect friend, perfect employee, perfect everything—and I longed for a husband just like him.

I would while away the hours picturing in my mind the magical moment my Prince Charming and I would meet. We would be at a fancy cocktail party. I would be impeccably dressed in a lovely white satin and lace minidress, platform shoes, perfectly coiffed hair, a splash of Charlie perfume, and just the right touch of makeup. He would mysteriously appear in a white leisure suit open at the neck, a single gold chain gracing his bare chest, and the subtle scent of English Leather announcing his presence. Our eyes would meet across the crowded room. We would fall instantly and passionately in love. He would be drop-dead gorgeous and have enough money to support me in the manner to which I wanted to become accustomed. What a wild imagination I had!

Unfortunately, our actual introduction wasn't nearly as romantic as that. We met in a bar while I was home from college for the weekend. We each arrived with a friend in tow, hoping to meet just the right dance partner for the evening. Coincidentally, our friends happened to know each other, so we found a table together and ordered a round of drinks. I quickly noticed that one of the guys had a Band-Aid around his ring finger—a poor cover-up for the fact that he was married. But I didn't care. I had my sights set on his friend anyway.

Forty-three years later, I can still picture my Prince Charming like it was yesterday. I couldn't take my eyes off him. He was the most handsome man I had ever seen. There he sat in his blue flower print silk shirt, suede jacket, and slightly flared jeans, his gorgeous, wavy hair gently brushing his shoulders. He even bore my brother's name—Gary Lee. How could it get better than that? I don't know if I would say it was love at first sight, but it was most definitely *deep like*.

The four of us spent the first hour or so getting to know one another. I, however, loved to dance and waited not so patiently for my handsome prince to whisk me off to the dance floor. Instead, his married friend kept asking me. Each time, I would glance over at Gary, hoping he would rescue me, but he said nothing. After a while, I relented and danced with Bob—at arm's length.

The evening wore on, and though Gary and I were making a lovely connection, he never once asked me to dance. Just when I had about run out of hope, we suddenly found ourselves alone at the table. By that time, I had enough liquor in me to cover any insecurities I had been experiencing all night long. So, I leaned forward, batting my baby-blue eyes, and with a boozy boldness announced, "You know, Gary, I've been waiting all night for you to ask me to dance." To which he replied, "I thought you wanted to be with Bob." What could I do but throw my head back and laugh.

We danced the rest of the night away, barely taking our eyes off each other. When it was time to part for the evening, we stood at the doorway wrapped in a sweet embrace for the longest time. Neither of us wanted to let go. Looking back at that tender moment, I can't help but smile, knowing God had a plan much greater than our imaginings. Within the year, we were married!

Life together was everything we had hoped it would be ... at least in the beginning. I thought I had finally found the one thing that would make me feel good about myself. Yet it wasn't long before those old familiar insecurities returned. I couldn't help but wonder what I was missing that even being married to the man of my dreams couldn't seem to fix.

The only thing that made any sense was the fact that I had always wanted to be a mother. *That's it! We need a baby!* Before we could barely blink, I was pregnant. What a joy it was carrying that precious little one!

Our son's entry into the world was a difficult twenty-six-hour journey. Despite that, nothing could compare to the feeling that washed over me as I gazed into his beautiful face, and he wrapped his little arms right around my heart. I had never felt such love. Michael, our firstborn—a little piece of Gary and a little piece of me—specially delivered just for us by a God I believed existed but knew very little about.

Gary and I had decided from day one that if we were blessed with children, I would leave my day job and stay home to raise our little ones. Oh, how I loved being that precious boy's mommy! But children grow, and it wasn't long before he didn't need me the same way anymore.

What is wrong with me? I have everything I ever wanted. Why do I feel so empty?

The answer seemed simple enough though. I just needed another baby. After all, Michael was already two. That was it! Once again, pregnancy was an easy accomplishment. Those nine months sped quickly by as we waited with great anticipation for our newest bundle of joy. I was absolutely convinced that his or her arrival on the scene would make all the difference for me. And it did … at least for a while. Yet that old familiar unrest settled in before our sweet baby, Scott, was even six months old. I loved those boys and their wonderful father with all my heart and couldn't imagine what could possibly be missing that left me in this state. *Maybe this is just a normal, temporary thing— perhaps some form of postpartum depression.* The weeks slipped by, and I was no closer to wholeness than I had been months before. Something had to be done. But what? One bright Sunday morning, as I was letting our dog out for a romp, the steeple of the little white church down the road caught my eye. I stood for the longest time watching the line of cars pulling into the parking lot. The church was just a few doors away, and I could hear laughter and the voices of people greeting one another as they strolled into the familiar building together. What did they have that I didn't? I observed from a distance, wishing I could be part of them as envy enveloped me.

The memory of a similar little white church from years gone by graced my thoughts, bringing a smile to my face. It was Children's Day. Every pew was filled with proud moms, dads and grandparents. All the kids were gathered in the fellowship hall, anxiously awaiting their turn in the spotlight. Each of us was expected to sing, play an instrument, or recite a poem at this special event. I, however, would be performing all three. There I stood in my Sunday finest—long blond ringlets cascading down the back of my white eyelet dress, brand-new patent leather shoes, and a smile as big as all outdoors. Unlike the rest of the crowd, I wasn't the least bit nervous. After all, my daddy was in the audience. At the ripe old age of four, I knew he would always be there for me, that he would always be proud of me.

Tears streamed down my face as the memories of that day made me long for the innocence I had long since lost and the loving-kindness that once defined church for me. I wanted desperately to recapture those feelings. Somewhere deep in my hurting soul was the slightest hope that it could be possible. But how?

With each passing Sunday, my desire to somehow reexperience my childhood church days grew. I would find myself watching the clock and wondering what I was missing when I knew the worship service was going on without me. Yet, becoming one of those "church folks" didn't really appeal to me either. Then I would gaze into the faces of my beautiful little boys and wonder if I was doing the right thing. Wouldn't good parents take their children to church? I had no idea how my husband would feel since we rarely discussed anything of a spiritual nature. Little did I know, the Holy Spirit was wooing both of us, preparing us for a life we never could have foreseen. By the time I gathered enough courage to speak with him about it, God had been moving in his heart as well, and we agreed it was time for us to take our boys to church. We, however, came up with what we thought was a brilliant plan. We would go to church as a family and make sure our children were in Sunday school every week. But we were not getting involved in any other church stuff.

The next Sunday, with our boys and a bit of anxiety in tow, we ventured out on our first visit to our little neighborhood church. The congregation seemed so warm and welcoming, and I wanted whatever it was they had. Though I had no idea what that meant, I wanted it just the same. Before I knew what was happening, I found myself involved in all kinds of what I referred to as "activities" in the church. I was so happy. But while my spirits were soaring, Gary was increasingly concerned. "What are you doing? We said we weren't going to get involved in that church stuff." I had simply moved on to plan B. He was still on plan A.

We had been attending regularly for a few months when the church hosted what they called a spiritual life retreat. I had no idea what that was. All I knew was that my new friends would be there. What fun! I could never have anticipated what the Lord had in store for me there though.

The retreat was held in the fellowship hall of the church. I walked toward the circle of chairs with great excitement, ready for a fun weekend. Instead, God met me the moment I entered the room. My ears picked up the familiar words of a song I had come to know very well. "Seek ye first the kingdom of God." At the time,

I didn't even realize those words were in the Bible, Matthew chapter 6, verse 33 to be exact (KJV). People were standing around talking with one another, while I found myself in my own little world. My whole body began to shake.

What in the world is happening?

Just then, the retreat leader (a woman from Long Island I had yet to meet) locked eyes with me, crossed the room, and stood directly in front of me. I couldn't help but wonder what this stranger was doing. My heart raced as she gently laid her hand on my shoulder and asked a question that left me speechless. "If the living Christ was standing this close to you, what would you do?" I stared at her for what seemed like an eternity, feeling as though I were looking right into the face of God. I couldn't answer her. I had no words but instead melted to the floor in a heap, unable to control my emotions.

That wise woman turned to the rest of the people and sweetly announced, "Folks, I realize we haven't begun our retreat yet, but this young lady and I need to have a little chat." She gently helped me to my feet, took my hand, and led me to the top of the stairs. There she opened her Bible and read to me from a passage I had never heard before. "If you confess with your mouth Jesus as Lord, and believe in your heart that God raised Him from the dead, you will be saved" (Romans 10:9 NASB). I was speechless.

I had been calling myself a Christian, believing that title was earned through church attendance, that I was saved. Oh, how wrong I was! That night, seated in a stairwell with the most Christlike person I had ever met, I confessed my sins to God and accepted Jesus as my Lord and Savior. That God-shaped hole in my heart was finally filled.

I spent the next two weeks reading the Bible and praying what I thought at the time were feeble prayers. My new life in Christ was just beginning, and I could hardly control my excitement. But then the unthinkable happened. My father-in-law died unexpectedly at the age of fifty-six. Everything in our world was suddenly turned upside down. Being the oldest boy in the family, my husband felt the weight of responsibility to take care of his mother. He never took the time to grieve but instead stepped right into his father's footsteps. Just like his dad, he became an alcoholic and an abuser.

At first, I thought it would be a temporary thing—that this was a part of the grieving process for him, and he would eventually get over it. Yet that didn't happen. With each passing day, he seemed worse, and the joy I had experienced when I first came to faith in Christ was all but gone. Not wanting to tarnish his reputation, I told no one but instead kept all my emotions bottled up inside. Fear and hopelessness were my constant companions, and I had no idea what to do about that. Many were the nights I would cry out to God, wondering where He was. I had given my life to Him. How could He allow this to happen to me?

As the years dragged on, I sank deeper and deeper into a pit of despair. We continued to go to church together, and each week I would put on my biggest, bravest smile that told the world I was fine. Yet in my heart of hearts, in the dark corners no one could see, I was so very broken. Part of me hoped that somebody, anybody would see through the facade I had created and help me. I had become an expert at hiding my feelings though, and no one was the wiser.

I tried to escape on several occasions. But each time I was set to put my plan into action, something drastic would happen to keep me firmly planted where I was. There seemed to be no hope of getting away from the horror that had become my life. I gave up all hope the day my dad was rushed to the hospital with a severe heart condition that required emergency bypass surgery. Any joy I once possessed was completely shattered.

Though my boys were my world, I was so low I honestly thought they would be better off without me. God had made a colossal mistake in creating me. My mother was right. I would never be enough.

Death seemed the only answer. Committing suicide would destroy my children, so it had to look like an accident. I came up with what seemed to be the perfect plan in my warped way of thinking. I would simply drive off a cliff. No drugs. No weapons. Just a car wreck. I even saw myself slamming on the brakes, intentionally creating skid marks that would leave the appearance that I had swerved to miss something.

The very night I was going to implement my plan, my best friend stopped by unannounced—something she never did. My first thought was, *Oh, great. What is she doing here?* I didn't want her to know what I was thinking. She would try to stop me, and that simply could not happen. There we were, standing in my driveway talking about something totally meaningless when the color drained out of her face. She grabbed me by the shoulders and, with tears streaming down her face, said with such desperation, "Gena, you can't do this! You can't do this!"

I had said absolutely nothing that would tip her off, yet somehow she knew. But I played dumb. "What? Can't do what?" I asked.

She looked at me with such love and concern, her voice trembling as she spoke what I knew were God's words to me. "I know what you're thinking of doing. This is not God's plan, Gena. This is not God's plan! Think of your children! This is not God's plan!"

A picture of my sons instantly popped into my head, and I began to sob uncontrollably. "What was I thinking? What was I thinking?" I cried. In that moment, I knew beyond a shadow of a doubt that God had intervened. He had spared my life for some reason I couldn't begin to understand.

At that time, I was attending a Bible study at the home of a couple in our neighborhood. My dirty laundry was well hidden from those dear people … or so I thought. Upon arrival one night, however, they revealed the truth. I was escorted to an empty seat right next to the group's leader. The silence in the room was almost deafening. I looked from face to face, trying to figure out what was happening. In each expression, there was a profound sense of concern. Our teacher took my hand and proceeded to tell me that they all knew what was happening in my home, that the Holy Spirit had spoken to them. Since that day, this band of prayer warriors had been lifting prayers of protection for my children and me and praying for my husband's salvation. Unbeknownst to me, they had been called by God to intervene. I could hardly believe what I was hearing.

God must really care about me. Maybe I really am enough.

Though I had no idea what the future might hold, an unexplainable peace settled on me, and I knew everything was going to be all right.

Years passed with no visible signs of change. Nevertheless, somewhere deep in my soul, I knew the Lord was at work, and I couldn't give up hope. Over time, as my faith grew, my joy slowly began to return. With every frightening moment, I found myself repeating over and over, "Nothing is impossible with God. Nothing is impossible with God." Somehow, I knew this was not going to last forever. Oh, it would take a miracle, all right, but I believed with everything in me that one day Gary was going to come to faith in Christ, and he would finally be healed.

I'd like to say that this newfound trust filled my heart with joy with every breath, but that simply would not be true. In the most difficult of moments, I still had to struggle through an overwhelming sense of fear before I remembered God's faithfulness and could pray my way out of it, despite what I was experiencing.

We were in the habit of sitting in the front pew at church since my husband believed if he sat that close to the pastor, it would guarantee him a seat in heaven. I have no idea where he came up with that notion, but he was totally convinced of its truth. My friends and I had been praying for what seemed like an eternity for Gary to come to his senses (my words, not theirs). One of the senior saints in our Bible study repeatedly tried to reassure me by reminding me of his own sister who had prayed for him for forty years before he came to faith in Christ. Every time he spoke the words "forty years," my stomach would flip. Though I smiled on the outside, everything in me screamed, *Forty years? Lord, I can't take that! You know I can't take that!* I could almost feel my joy slipping away again as my heart sank with every word. Each time, I fought to regain my footing and the spiritual progress I had made. I wondered how God would ever be able to soften such a hard heart. How? The dramatic answer to that question came much later—but thankfully, not forty years.

We continued to go to church and sat in our self-assigned front-row seats. Each week, I would pray for a miracle, but I saw no progress. Some days, discouragement clung to my hurting soul like a virus, infecting my every thought. I had been taught that joy should not depend on circumstances, that true joy comes only from Jesus. I had come to dearly love the Lord, but my struggle with my emotions was still so real. Would I ever be able to conquer this? Was my faith simply too small?

I had convinced myself that no one would ever understand this. So I breathed not a word to anyone but instead chose what seemed to be the next best option. I made a trip to the local Christian bookstore and looked for something to *fix* myself. After what seemed like hours of searching, I came up empty-handed and decided to abort the mission. But as I was headed for the door, a pink book with large letters and a rather goofy-looking cartoon of a woman on the cover caught my eye: *Pain is Inevitable, but Misery is Optional, so Stick a Geranium in Your Hat and Be Happy* by Barbara Johnson. I chuckled to myself and thought,

Wait ... you mean I simply need to choose *joy? Could it really be that simple?* The book just happened to be on sale. I bought it, hoping the breakthrough I'd been looking for would be contained within its pages. Reading the story of this amazing woman's journey filled me with hope, and I realized that pain really is inevitable, but misery is optional. I had a choice. I really had a choice. I wasn't a failure. I wasn't wrong. I was a human being with feelings like everyone else. But I was also a Christian with the best resources in the world contained between the pages of the Word of God. I could have joy. I just had to choose it. Simple, right? Wrong!

A lifetime of striving had taught me one thing. I had no idea how to make myself have joy. I had gotten very good at putting on a brave front. Yet my moods, my attitude, and my happiness were all still dependent upon my circumstances. I had pleaded with God on more occasions than I care to count to just give me joy. That's all I asked. Just give me joy. I wanted desperately to believe that I could have it, that it was mine for the taking. Unfortunately, there was still a part of me that thought I didn't deserve it, that this was my punishment.

It wasn't until the summer of 1993 that I finally understood. I had been invited to attend a conference at Gordon-Conwell Theological Seminary in Boston titled "Worship to Witness Through the Power of the

Holy Spirit." Though I had no idea what I was getting into, something in my spirit told me God would be waiting for me there.

I arrived at the college with a sense of excitement. The very first session began with what they called *worship*. Now, mind you, I had my own definition of that word. I thought worship was what we did on Sunday mornings in our little country church, contained in that building. And I was good at that. But this ... this was something completely foreign to me. People weren't just singing. They were raising their hands in praise and seemed to have a relationship with God that was much deeper than mine. I desperately wanted that.

When the keynote speaker stood to begin his teaching, a hush fell over the crowd. Everything in me resonated with his words. "Worship changes the worshipper into the image of the one worshipped." That was the key! Worship! I spent the rest of the weekend hanging on every word and learning the meaning of true worship. Though nothing about my circumstances had changed, something in me had. The Holy Spirit was alive and well in me. I was starting to understand that true joy really is formed amid difficult seasons. I could have that joy despite any wrong I had done or what was happening around me. I would always find it in the presence of God.

$\mathcal{T}$ime *to* $\mathcal{R}$eflect

In 1971, the beauty care company L'Oréal announced its new slogan, "Because I'm worth it." Though it may sound self-centered and even a bit egotistical, there is an element of truth in that statement. You, my friend, are worthy of joy because God wants nothing but the very best for you. To Him, you are most definitely worth it.

All too often, however, we get caught up in the lies we've been told, painful memories of our past mistakes, or the struggle to maintain our faith through the hardships of life. This can leave us feeling as though we are disqualified from experiencing any real joy. Oh, dear one, God wants you whole, filled with His joy. Of that I am certain.

You might have found in the pages of this chapter something that parallels your own life: areas you've kept hidden, emotions you've buried alive. Rest assured, though the truth may be hidden from the rest of the world, God knows. And He wants to set you free—free to experience all the joy that is yours in His presence.

I'd like to take you on a little journey now, one I pray will bring you to a place of peace and joy.

Picture yourself resting by a lovely mountain stream. You sit ever so quietly, enjoying the beauty of God's handiwork all around you. The brook babbles in delight as its playful waters tumble over smooth, flat stones and bright green, moss-covered rocks. A gentle breeze blows through the trees, the leaves twirling and swaying in rhythm with each breath of wind. You listen intently to the magnificent tones whistling through the branches, almost as if they have a language all their own. There's a peace in this lovely place, a peace that passes all understanding.

You're suddenly aware that you're not alone, but you're not the least bit frightened—because it's Him, it's Jesus. He sits down next to you, uttering not a word. His silence is a bit unnerving at first, but it takes only a moment for you to adjust to the quiet. Time seems to stand still as you simply enjoy His presence.

After a while, He rises to His feet, and you find yourself wanting to scream, "No! Please don't go yet!" But the words seem to stick in your throat. He reaches behind you and effortlessly lifts a very large yet lightweight black sack. You sit motionless for a moment, realizing it's the same bag you had been dragging along behind you for as long as you can remember. But how could that be? Your bag had become so heavy; it was almost impossible to bear the weight of it. Yet to Jesus it was as light as a feather. He motions for you to look inside. You hesitate, knowing its contents all too well. You look up at Jesus and see a love in His eyes you've never experienced anywhere else, and somehow you know everything is going to be okay. You lean forward and peer into the sack. It's full of rocks—big, heavy rocks. Each one bears a single word—fat, ugly, stupid, unfaithful, liar, abuser, idolater, selfish, bigot, and so on. It makes you sick to have to see them, yet you know you must. When you look back at Jesus, He's holding his arms out in front of Him, waiting for you to place these broken pieces of your life in His hands. Without a word, you begin the process, one rock at a time, tears trickling down your careworn face. As you place the last rock in His hands, He slowly turns toward the sun and without a word tosses your heavy burdens into the air. The two of you watch in silence as they float upward, gliding on the wind until they are completely out of sight. He turns to you and takes your hands in His—His touch a balm to your hurting soul. And then He speaks the three words that change your life forever, "It is finished" (John 19:30 NLT). He squeezes your hands as the most beautiful smile you have ever seen crosses His face. You know in that instant that no truer words were ever spoken. Because of Jesus, you can truly have joy.

I pray that God, the source of hope, will fill you
completely with joy and peace because you trust
in him. Then you will overflow with confident
hope through the power of the Holy Spirit.
—Romans 15:13 NLT

Dear God, thank You for Your grace that has given me
what I don't deserve. Thank You for Your mercy that
has *not* given me what I *do* deserve. I am so grateful
that You have called me out of darkness into Your
marvelous light (1 Pet. 2:9 NASB). Lord, I give You
all the broken pieces—everything that has stolen my
joy in the past. Thank You for removing each one of
them. Thank You for forgiving me and never again
remembering my sins (Heb. 8:12 NLT). How blessed
I am to know that when I confess my sins to You, You
remove them as far from me as the east is from the
west (Psalm 103:12 NLT). Help me to remember the
joy I can always find in Your presence, no matter what
is happening in my life at the time.

$\mathscr{P}eace$

God's sovereignty has not been
shipwrecked by your storm.
—Priscilla Shirer

There are certain moments in life that simply take
us by surprise. An unexpected visit from a long-lost
friend, a meteor shower, or a "just because I love you"
present bring a wonderful sense of delight. Then there
are the times that our hearts are not ready for. Crises
throw us off balance. We find ourselves in a state of
disbelief and shock, wondering where our next breath
will come from.

When our sons were young, I loved to think about
who they would become, what they would find to
do for a living, who they would marry, what their
children would be like, and where they would live. I
could hardly wait to see how they would use the gifts

God had given them. In all my musings, however, the thought never occurred to me that life might not be as lovely as my dreams for them.

By the time the boys hit their teen years, it was evident they probably weren't going to turn out like I thought. The older they got, the crazier their ideas became—at least that's how they appeared to their extremely overprotective mom. Our firstborn, Mike, thought living the life of a heavy metal rock star sounded like a good plan. Fame, fortune, and fun were his goals. Those "wild" ideas were certainly not on my radar for him. So I chose to think of it as a phase, something he would hopefully outgrow. His dreams of grandeur eventually faded away, though it was a very slow process.

His brother, Scott, on the other hand, started down a path that seemed right and good, absolutely perfect for him. From the time he was a little boy, he had this insatiable desire to build and fix things and could find his way around his dad's toolbox far better than I. Even as a youngster, he was always working on some kind of project. After high school, he entered the workforce as a mason. Though he excelled in his work, he couldn't seem to find happiness in it. I gave his uneasiness little thought because, after all, he was a baby adult. Sometimes it takes years of experience, trial, and error to figure out what you really want to do for the rest of your life. As time wore on, his attitude only seemed to worsen, and my concern for him deepened.

In the spring of 2001, two years after his graduation, he walked in the door, looked me square in the eye, and uttered words I will never forget. "Oh, by the way, Mom, there's a marine recruiter coming here tomorrow."

I stared at him in disbelief, completely dumbstruck. *The marines? What?* They had been trying to recruit him for two years. Each time they called, he would politely turn them down, hang up the phone, and, with a chuckle, insist he would never do anything that stupid. But something had changed. The look on his face told me he was serious, though I didn't want to believe it. Somehow, I managed to catch my breath enough to ask the question for which I really didn't want an answer. "Son ... are you actually considering this?"

He answered with all sincerity, "Yeah, Mom, I am." His reasoning? He was in a dead-end job, and the world was at peace. To him, the timing could not have been more perfect.

I held onto the dining room chair for support, trying to compose myself, knowing the importance of the right response. I had always supported our fighting men and women in every way. But not my son! My old enemy, fear, instantly invaded my space, and I found myself consumed with anxiety. I knew the marines touted the phrase "First to Fight," so I came up with every conceivable reason for him to explore other branches of the service. Yet try as I might, Scott wouldn't budge. His mind was set.

The next day, a recruiter did indeed show up at our house. Before I knew what was happening, my boy was heading out the door with a marine who would soon be considered his comrade in arms. My heart was broken. I dropped to my knees and, with tears streaming down my face, prayed for God's intervention.

Each minute felt like hours as I waited for their return. I wanted desperately for Scott to walk in the door saying he'd changed his mind, that this just wasn't for him. Yet somewhere deep in my soul, I knew his decision had already been made. My son was soon to become a marine.

It was late in the afternoon before the two resurfaced. Scott was proudly sporting a black T-shirt with four bold white letters on it—USMC. He could hardly contain his excitement. I knew how important my support was to him. As difficult as it was, I smiled bravely, congratulated him, gave him a big hug, told him how proud I was of him, and tried not to get sick. My son was about to be known as one of the few, the proud, a marine. And there was absolutely nothing I could do about it.

The days flew by as Scott trained on his own, hoping to prepare himself for the rigors of boot camp.

As excited as he was, however, I sensed a nervousness beginning to creep in with each passing day. Was he questioning his decision? There was no turning back. He had signed on the dotted line. For the next eight years, he belonged to the US Marine Corps.

After weeks of waiting, the day finally arrived for him to begin this new chapter in his life. Scott's recruiter arrived early in the morning to take him to Syracuse, where he would board a bus bound for boot camp on Parris Island, South Carolina. Everything in me wanted to grab my lanky 6'2" son and lock him in his room! But I knew I could no longer protect him.

The entire family huddled together in the driveway. We were hanging on to one another for dear life, not wanting to let go. This would be the last time we would all be together for three long months. There wasn't a dry eye as each one of us fought to deal with our own emotions. Just minutes later, I stood silently watching as my son drove away to a world fraught with danger.

A million pictures of my little boy ran through my mind. The day I found out I was expecting him, his miraculous entry into the world, building snowmen in the backyard, his first day of school, watching him pitch a no-hitter in Little League, his first girlfriend, graduation day, and so on. Where had the time gone? I knew in my heart that from that day forward, nothing would ever be the same.

Time dragged as I anxiously awaited his weekly

letters. Though his notes were always filled with news, I found myself trying to read between the lines, wondering what he might be keeping to himself. I worried over the silliest things. He was such a sound sleeper. How would they ever wake him up in the morning? I pictured his sergeant screaming through a bullhorn to blast him out of bed. And they would expect him to be organized. Scott? My Scott? What about his personality? Always the jokester, he was the life of the party at home. What would they have to do to break him of that? Would there be any semblance of my unpredictable, fun-loving, wacky boy left? Thankfully, my mind stayed in that realm through the twelve long weeks of his boot camp experience. My mother's heart simply would not allow me to think what the future might hold for my son as a marine.

He sailed through boot camp with the greatest of ease—at least that's what he wanted us to believe. He griped about the heat, fleas, and being exhausted. That was about the extent of his complaints. So I convinced myself that he was still the same crazy guy, with a few more muscles and maybe a tattoo.

I counted down the days until his graduation. After all, three months is an awfully long time for a mother to be separated from her son; at least it was for this mama. His father and I arrived at Parris Island on what I thought was an unusually hot, muggy day. Apparently, most of the summer had been plagued with extreme heat and oppressive humidity. My mind raced. *Poor Scott. How did he ever survive ten-mile hikes in this kind of weather? Was he okay?*

We spent the first day touring the depot, witnessing recruit life firsthand. There were young men and women in various phases of their training everywhere we looked. As fascinating as it was, I just wanted to see my son. Toward the end of the tour, the driver stopped the bus, looked over his shoulder, and announced, "If you look out the back window, you'll see your marines practicing for graduation tomorrow." There they were, all lined up on the sidewalk, as stiff as statues, each one a carbon copy of the one next to him. Much to my surprise, we were allowed to get off the bus, with strict instructions to refrain from contact of any kind with the recruits. Filled with excitement, we darted off the bus as if our lives depended on it. We approached the sea of uniformed marines with utmost respect. Their very presence seemed to command that. After a few moments of searching, we spotted Scott. It took but a glance to realize he had changed. In three short months, our boy had become a man.

Graduation day was filled with all the pomp and circumstance we had anticipated. After all, this was the culmination of months of discipline and hard work. The bleachers were filled with family and friends, each waiting expectantly to greet their marine after the long weeks of separation.

As the boot camp survivors marched onto the hundred-plus-degree parade deck, I was amazed at their precision—every step in perfect sync with one another. They had become a well-oiled machine and were a part of something much greater than themselves. My heart swelled with pride, knowing my son was now a member of this illustrious team.

The ceremony was beyond impressive. I told myself to memorize every moment, knowing it was one of those occasions that would only pass my way once. But if the truth be known, I was just about jumping out of my skin waiting to hug my boy's neck!

After what seemed like hours, the mass of family and friends that had gathered for graduation was finally allowed to greet our marines. Everyone appeared to wait patiently for their turn to exit the bleachers and begin the search for their loved one. Everyone, it seemed, except me. Suddenly, I spotted Scott in that sea of marines, and every ounce of common sense left my body! Without a moment's hesitation, I wiggled my way through the crowd, skipping as many steps as I dared on the way, and jumped right over the rope railing to get to him. It never once occurred to me that probably wasn't the best option. Surprisingly enough, no one even tried to stop me. Considering the number of marines Parris Island had graduated, I'm guessing there had to be at least one or two overly excited moms over the years who simply could not control their enthusiasm.

I ran to my son, wrapping my arms around his waist—his much thinner waist. *How could he possibly be this skinny? What did they do to my boy?* All I wanted to do was protect him, yet I knew I couldn't. In that instant, I prayed for the world to remain at peace—at least for eight years.

The trip home was nothing like I'd anticipated. I pictured Scott talking nonstop, telling us every little detail of his experience. Instead, he was pensive, almost distant. He stood taller and straighter, with a sense of pride and confidence I'd never seen in him. But his sense of humor, always his trademark, was gone, along with a piece of my heart.

How blessed we were to have our son home on leave for ten days! After that, he attended the Marine Corps School of Infantry in Maryland, followed by Military Occupational Training in California. The fact that he was now a fighting man unnerved me to the core of my being. What would be expected of him?

He had no sooner finished his training when the unthinkable happened. On September 11, 2001, nineteen al-Qaeda terrorists staged a well-organized attack on the United States under the leadership of Osama bin Laden. They hijacked four American planes filled with enough fuel for a cross-country trip. Two smashed into the Twin Towers in New York City, one into the Pentagon, and one missed its target all together because of the bravery of its passengers. This was war.

A month later, the United States invaded Afghanistan. The purpose was to dismantle al-Qaeda and remove the Taliban from power. I prayed with every breath that the marines being sent there wouldn't include my son and thanked God with each passing day that kept him stateside.

I told myself I should be able to maintain my peace. After all, Jesus said, "Peace I leave with you; my peace I give you. I do not give to you as the world gives. Do not let your hearts be troubled and do not be afraid" (John 14:27 NIV). I would repeat that verse over and over again throughout the day. But as the war in Afghanistan heated up, my worry increased, and the peace that had once come easily for me was rapidly evaporating.

I hadn't even come to grips with the reality of this horror when we received word from Scott that he was being deployed to Iraq. *Oh, God, no! How could this be happening? Not my boy! Please, Lord, not my boy!*

I clung to the hope that God would somehow intervene and that justice would be served without war having to be a part of it—ever. I had no idea how that could happen, but it was all I had to hang on to.

It was on a cold Thursday morning, March 20, 2003, that my world and everything in me was rocked to the core. War had begun. At first, I was glued to the television, watching in shock and disbelief. I had prayed with every fiber of my being for God to stop this madness before it even began. The problem was my heart simply wouldn't accept anything else. Never once did I pray for God's will. The thought that His will might include this war was beyond the realm of my imagination. When my brain and heart finally caught up with reality, I was devastated. Didn't God hear me? Was my faith too small?

I spent the next six months engulfed in fear. I knew my son was in a kill-or-be-killed situation, and I couldn't protect him. I tried to combat those feelings with scriptures on fear, but nothing seemed to be helping. I was buried in worry, and I couldn't seem to find my way out.

It wasn't until I heard a teaching on the ninety-first psalm that I had any semblance of peace. I began reading and rereading aloud that beautiful poem of protection many times a day. Much to my surprise, I started to sense the presence of the Holy Spirit with each reciting, and His peace would descend on me. God was slowly chipping away at the fear in this frightened mom's hurting soul. It wasn't long before I had committed that powerful Word to memory. It was the only place I found comfort throughout the duration of Scott's deployment.

I wish I could say God removed all fear during that

time. The truth is, though, it wasn't until I was able to wrap my arms around my son again that I had total peace. If this was a test, I certainly didn't fare very well. Yet I have the assurance that the Lord knows my heart, and the recognition of my shortcomings did more for my spiritual growth than if He had simply taken my fear away. I learned so much about myself in those six months. More importantly, I experienced God's unconditional love as I struggled with my feelings. He taught me that He is greater than my worried heart, bigger than my anxieties. If I trust in that and in the power of His Word, I can find peace knowing that His sovereignty is not shipwrecked by my storm.

Time to Reflect

We live in a day and age when a measure of fear lives in the hearts of many people. Some would say if we call ourselves believers, we should never experience fear because it means we don't trust God. Perhaps that's what you've been taught. But I'd like to challenge your way of thinking for a moment. Why would God go to all the trouble of addressing that subject so many times if we were never going to experience that emotion? I believe His purpose in telling us repeatedly not to fear is simply to remind us that in the midst of whatever it is that evokes that emotion in us, He's got us. He'll never desert us. When I read the words in Isaiah 41:10 from the NIV, "So do not fear for I am with you; do not be dismayed, for I am your God," I don't hear him yelling at me. I know some people do. They hear those words as a command. *Do not fear!* That's not what I hear. What I receive in my spirit when I read those words is something like, "It's okay, honey. You don't have to be afraid. I'm right here." He's not chastising me. He's comforting me, reassuring me that even in those moments when I'm afraid and I can't see Him, I can trust His heart.

Few things make us feel more vulnerable than fear.

It keeps us from enjoying life the way God intended. It holds us back from being all He's calling us to be. It is a bitter root that robs us of our peace. So let me ask you. Is there something stirring in your soul that you would love to pursue, but you're afraid—afraid of failing, afraid of succeeding, afraid of what others might think, afraid of being noticed, afraid of rejection, afraid of the future, afraid of the unknown? Is your fear for a loved one consuming you? What is it that's holding you back? What's stealing your peace?

Give yourself some space now to be alone with God. Take your time. Rest assured, He is in no hurry. As a matter of fact, He's been waiting for this moment. It's time, my friend—time for you to face those fears and give them to the One who dearly wants to carry them for you. Oh, how He loves you!

Give all your worries and cares to
God, for he cares about you.
—1 Peter 5:7 NLT

Gracious Lord, how thankful I am that You have a plan for my life that's good, plans to prosper me and not to harm me (Jer. 29:11 NIV). I know You are for me, and You have only my best interests at heart. But I've let my fears get in the way of Your good and perfect will for my life. I know that You did not give me a spirit of fear but of power and of love and of a sound mind (2 Tim. 1:7 NKJV). Please help me, God. I long to be all you're calling me to be—nothing more and nothing less. I give You every fear that's holding me captive. Thank You, Lord, for holding my hand as I walk this road, for never leaving me or forsaking me (Deut. 31:6 NIV). Thank You for your peace, which exceeds anything I can understand that guards my heart and mind as I live in Christ Jesus (Phil. 4:7 NLT). Oh, how I love You, my Lord and my God.

Patience

Patience is not just the ability to wait; it is the ability
to keep a good attitude while we are waiting.

—Joyce Meyer

Don't you just love sitting in the waiting room? If
you're like most people in this fast-paced world, you
responded with a resounding, "No!" Depending on
why you're in this holding tank, waiting might cause
you serious anxiety. It's hard to get cozy when you're
wondering how much your visit to the mechanic is
going to cost or what the doctor will find in your
medical tests, isn't it? Let's face it. The simple truth is
we spend a lot more time waiting for answers to our
questions than actually receiving them. My friend,
you'd best make yourself comfortable.

They say patience is a virtue. *Oxford's Living
Dictionary* defines it as "the capacity to accept or

tolerate delay, problems, or suffering without becoming annoyed or anxious." For the most part, that would seem to apply to me—at least on the surface. I'm generally not one who is easily angered or frustrated. I don't mind waiting in line. I think of it as a time to make new friends. Being cut off in traffic doesn't aggravate me. It's an opportunity to pray for the safety of all those on the road. Known as a peacemaker to many, I am often found in the middle of other people's woes. Consequently, the world would see me as a very patient person. And I am just that—with everyone except myself. Oh, I can generally tolerate delays or problems with an element of patience. But suffering? Now that's another story altogether.

Years ago, I walked through a period I now refer to as the winter of my soul. Prior to that time, I often found myself gazing out my dining room window in awe of God's handiwork, completely overwhelmed by the beauty and the splendor of His creation. Some would say I viewed the world with a childlike wonder, as though everything was a miracle. It was on a cold, snowy day that I realized something had changed. As I sat looking out that same window, my body racked with pain, I saw nothing but death—no flowers, no color, no animals, no birds—nothing but death. It was the winter of my soul.

So many questions invaded my once-trusting mind. *Why, God? Why is this happening to me? Why can't the doctors, these highly trained professionals, figure this out? How will my husband ever be able to stand in the gap and be both mother and father to our boys? You promised never to leave me or forsake me, God. Where are You?*

This illness had come on so quickly, without warning. One minute I was happily engrossed in all the preparations for Christmas; the next, I could barely stand. For the first time in my life, food had absolutely no appeal. I lost twenty-five pounds in a month's time. A combination of strange neurological abnormalities was occurring, and my body was rapidly deteriorating. What in the world was happening to me? Doctors ran every conceivable test trying to determine the source of these bizarre and widespread symptoms. Cancer, heavy metal poisoning, Lyme disease, MS, and a host of other ailments were systematically ruled out. Finally, completely baffled by this strange illness, my doctor asked me a question no one ever wants to hear. "Gena, do you think you could be imagining this?" It was in that moment I knew that, short of a miracle from God, I was going to die from something modern medicine couldn't diagnose. The trip home was a blur. There were no words. Just gut-wrenching sobs from the depth of my being.

Two days later, though there was still no change in my condition, I went to church with the conviction that God had the answer. What frightened me was the unknown. What form would healing take? Was He preparing me to meet Him far sooner than I would have dreamt?

As I sat in the pew of our little country church listening to others share their joys and concerns, something stirred in me. Up until that point, it was a rarity for me to let others know I was standing in the need of prayer. After all, I was the one people came to, the strong, patient one, the prayer warrior, the woman of great faith.

For a reason unknown to me at the time, I felt an urgency to share with these, my friends, what had been happening to me. Clutching my Bible in my trembling hands, I poured out my heart and let them into this nightmare that had become my life. It was then that God clearly spoke to me—not in an audible voice but in a way that touched my very soul. I turned to the book of James and tearfully read the passage from the fifth chapter, verses 14 and 15. "Is anyone among you sick? Let them call the elders of the church to pray over them and anoint them with oil in the name of the Lord. And the prayer offered in faith will make the sick person well; the Lord will raise them up. If they have sinned, they will be forgiven" (NIV). Looking into the faces of these faithful believers, I saw nothing but the deepest love and concern. With a boldness I never knew I possessed, I spoke these words, "If any of you are true believers in the Word of God and the power in the blood that Jesus shed for our healing, I'd like to ask you to join me at the altar after the service." Our pastor, a man so very sensitive to the spirit of God, stopped the service and invited me to come forward right then and there. With my husband holding me up on one side and my best friend on the other, we knelt at the altar. As the pastor anointed me with oil and uttered a prayer of faith for my healing, the entire congregation came forward to lay hands on me. Those who couldn't reach directly, laid hands on the person in front of them communicating agreement and encouragement. The power of God fell in such a mighty way that when I rose from the altar, I knew something profound had just happened. Though my physical body felt no different, something stirred in my spirit.

Suddenly, the front door of the church opened. A mysterious stranger, looking to be in his mid-thirties walked down the center aisle, never taking his eyes off me. I found myself wondering who this man was and why I felt moved to tears when our eyes met. He walked directly up to me and announced, "I have a message for you from God. Because of your faith and the faith of your friends, God has chosen to begin the healing process. It won't look like a miracle since healing will not be instantaneous. You'll show some improvement, reach a plateau for a time, show further signs of recovery, and plateau again until you are well.

But rest assured you will regain full health." He smiled the warmest smile I had ever seen, turned, and left the building the same way he had come, never to be seen again.

I was standing there awestruck when my faithful friend ever so gently told me that God had spoken to her concerning me. Of course, my curiosity was piqued, but I never anticipated the words she would say. "There's somewhere I want to take you," she said through her tears. I'd been to so many professionals. What was she talking about? When she mentioned the town, I knew exactly who and what she meant. She wanted to take me to a local chiropractor who also dealt in holistic medicine. Knowing I would resist her efforts with everything in me, she said, "Gena, I'm watching you die right before my eyes. Please. I really believe God wants you to see him—that this man has your answer." Never doubting the depth of her faith, and feeling I had no other recourse, I reluctantly agreed.

Through a series of tests, this doctor quickly revealed the source of all my symptoms. I was beyond relieved that someone finally heard me and believed me, that this illness wasn't imaginary. But it was the words he spoke next that confirmed for me that God was and always will be in control. "This is how your healing will take place. You'll get better, you'll plateau, you'll get better, you'll plateau. But don't worry. You will regain your health." You can imagine the sense of awe and wonder I experienced at that moment. God had heard us! He really heard us! Over time, my body responded to treatment, improving exactly as the mysterious stranger had predicted. This doctor was the flesh and blood agent of the Lord's healing. I knew in my spirit that my suspicions were true. The mysterious stranger was sent by God almighty to deliver a message that blessed not only my life but the lives of the faithful in that little country church.

My patience had been tested beyond anything I thought I could endure. Was it pleasant? Absolutely not! The lessons learned during that time, however, have been worth any discomfort it caused me. When the mysterious stranger appeared out of nowhere, God proved to me that He had been there all the while, that He still loved me in spite of all my questions, that I can trust Him in my darkest moments. He is faithful to reveal His perfect plan in His perfect time, whether I'm patient in the waiting room or not.

Since then, I have faced several life-threatening illnesses. Yes, I still wrestle with some of the same emotions I experienced during the winter of my soul. There are still times when I think I just can't take another step. But by taking the time to remember and meditate on the goodness of God, my perspective begins to change. I allow myself the privilege of getting comfortable in the waiting room and basking in His presence. It is there, in the secret place with God, that He reminds me that all things are possible with Him. And when I truly grab hold of that truth, I realize once again that patience is not just the ability to wait; it is the ability to keep a good attitude while I am waiting.

Time to Reflect

In the thirteenth chapter of 1 Corinthians, God's very first word choice to describe the unique nature of His love toward us is the word patient. "Love is patient" (NIV). In the original Greek, the type of love the writer is referring to is agape—the highest form of unconditional love; love for humankind, which finds its origin in God Himself. Phillip Yancey once said, "There is nothing we can do to make God love us more, and nothing we can do could make God love us less." It's the same kind of love that Jesus referred to when He commanded His followers in John 13:34–35, "Love one another. As I have loved you, so you must love one another. By this everyone will know that you are my disciples, if you love one another" (NIV). If we are ever to find victory in this area, we need to remind ourselves of how patient God has been with us, even in those times when we failed to love Him as we should. In order to be a reflection of His love, it's critical that we follow His example.

Have you ever asked anyone to pray that you will have patience in dealing with difficult people or situations? I used to be one who thought (and even said), "Oh, you don't want me to pray for patience. You won't like what God gives you to learn the lesson." Though I suppose there's an element of truth in that, time and experience have taught me it's still basically wrong thinking. Should we instead be asking Him to increase our love toward others as well as ourselves?

Take a sheet of paper and number it 1-10. On a scale of 1–10 (10 being best), how would you rate yourself and your patience level in the following areas:

1. When someone cuts you off in traffic
2. While waiting in line
3. With cranky neighbors
4. With your children
5. When someone's opinion is different from yours
6. When others differ with your interpretation of a Bible passage
7. When your church makes changes you don't agree with
8. When talking about politics
9. When speaking of religion
10. During times of suffering

Were you honest with yourself? Totally honest? Take a look at the list again. Ask God to reveal to you moments when your patience has been tested in these areas. Now try rating yourself again. How did you fare this time?

Turn your attention now to 1 Corinthians 13:4 and

repeat the first three words slowly until the truth in them saturates your soul. "Love is patient. Love is patient. Love is patient" (NLT). You are speaking of a piece of God's character, His very nature, a part He wants you to reflect to the world.

Perhaps you're someone who's struggled with this issue for as long as you can remember in one way or another. And you fear you will never be able to conquer it. My friend, don't believe the lies of the enemy! Philippians 4:13 reads, "I can do all things through Christ who strengthens me" (NKJV). That, dear one, is the truth. You can do this! But God doesn't expect you to do it alone. The presence and the power of the one who gave His life for you is all you need. Reach out to Him. He's waiting with open arms.

And now these three remain: faith, hope and
love. But the greatest of these is love.
—1 Cor. 13:13 NIV

Dear God, my patience runs thin more often than I want to admit. I'm ashamed of my behavior and thoughts. "But you, O Lord, are a God of compassion and mercy; slow to get angry and filled with unfailing love and faithfulness" (Psalm 86:15 NLT). Your Word says we don't have because we don't ask You. (James 4:2 NIV). So today I humbly ask You to forgive my impatience with others as well as with myself. Please, God, help me to love as You love. May my life be a reflection of You and only You.

$\mathscr{K}$*indness*

The smallest act of kindness is worth
more than the greatest intention.

—Kahlil Gibran

I don't know about you, but it always brings a smile
to my face when I hear of someone performing a
random act of kindness. Caring people have paid for
a stranger's dinner, rescued trapped animals, baked
cookies for shut-ins, and left encouraging notes on
napkins in restaurants. Selfless acts to spread a little
joy. Oh, what a beautiful place this world would be if
we woke up each day with the desire in our hearts to
make someone's day a little brighter. How I wish I had
come to this realization at a much younger age.

It seems like yesterday that I was a teenager. Yet
decades have come and gone. What a unique time
of life that is! You want to be treated like an adult,

but in reality, you're nowhere near ready for the responsibilities that come with that. You feel invincible and so very grown-up. You think of most adults (except the "cool" ones, of course) as clueless. You reason that what you lack in experience is more than compensated for in your level of intelligence. Therefore, it only makes sense that you should always put yourself first. After all, you deserve that.

Now before you come unglued, hear me out, would you? That scenario is not the case for every teenager. But it certainly describes me to a tee. I was involved in so many activities it would make the average person's head spin. That doesn't mean my choices were always right, though. Everything I chose to involve myself in was something that would ultimately make me happy. Yes, I was known for doing an occasional good deed, but it was usually with an ulterior motive. Before launching into a new venture, I would generally ask myself, "Will this make me more popular? Will it take me away from my friends and things I really want to do?" If I couldn't answer either of those questions to my satisfaction, it wasn't worth my time. Selfish? You bet I was.

It wasn't until I realized my self-centered attitude had seriously damaged someone I cared deeply about that I began to question what I was doing.

My parents had few of what I would consider real friends. Most of their time was spent with my mother's family. There were those, however, that they played cards with on occasion. One couple graced our home more frequently than the others. Their daughter, Debbie, was several years my junior and treated me as though I was a princess. I'd always wanted a little sister, so having her tag along was fun for a while. I would even visit her at home when she was ill, which seemed to be quite often. After all, she didn't have many friends. Or so I thought. I had only the purest of intentions in the beginning.

Debbie's attachment to me grew with each passing day. She needed me, and I knew it. However, my priorities didn't line up with hers. I wanted the memories of my senior year to be filled with friends and fun, not babysitting a clingy little kid who wasn't even related to me. A selfish teenage attitude began to replace the deep feelings I once had for her. My "busy" schedule conveniently got in the way. Over time, we lost touch altogether. I have no idea whatever became of her. Did I break her heart? Probably. All I know is that God gave me an opportunity to make a difference with this one small act of kindness, and I blew it. For years, I beat myself up over it.

Just when I thought I would never resolve this issue in my heart, I met Jenna. My husband and I had been asked to minister in song at a small country church a few hours from our home. As was our custom, we prayed for Jesus to hide us behind His cross so that others would be drawn to Him through the music and our testimonies. Minutes before we began, the side door opened as a large family entered the sanctuary. I quickly realized this was a unique group of people. Every child appeared to have some sort of special need. If there had been time to ponder this rarity at that moment, I'm sure I would have.

The whole evening, I found myself drawn to this family, feeling nothing but empathy for how difficult life must be for them. Little did I know, they had an understanding of God I had yet to grasp. As the concert drew to a close and folks gathered around to speak with us, the mother of all those dear children quietly approached and asked if I would join her in the back of the sanctuary. Surely, she wanted me to pray with her. I was prepared for that. Following her down the aisle to the very last pew, she introduced me to her daughter, Jenna. I hadn't seen this child during the concert because she was lying down. This beautiful girl was sixteen years old and only about three feet long, her body completely contorted. Her clouded blue eyes made me wonder what, if anything, she could see.

Her mother proceeded to tell me that each of their ten children were special needs kids. The couple knew early in their marriage that God had chosen them to raise a family of those considered *less than*, the most disabled lying in the pew in front of me. My heart was absolutely broken.

Why, God? Why?

In the moments that followed, that question was completely erased. What I didn't realize at first quickly became evident. Jenna didn't speak. Though I couldn't bring myself to ask, I wondered why her mother was so adamant about having me meet this particular child of hers. With tears in her eyes, Mom explained that every time her daughter heard my voice, she tried to sing along. I sat down next to Jenna and asked if she'd like to sing with me. The broadest smile I had ever seen crossed her sweet face, and my heart melted. For the next fifteen minutes or so, I held her hand as we sang together. Though she made nothing more than guttural sounds, with every breath, this broken child glorified God in a way that was greater than anything I had ever experienced before. It was a life-changing moment for me—the night God gave me a second chance.

Little did I know, meeting Jenna was only the beginning.

My husband and I had been traveling in music ministry for several years and had felt called by God to use the money we were given to make a difference in the world. There was so much need though. How would we ever be able to decide who to support? Knowing the Lord would make it clear to us, we began to pray. It took nearly a year for that prayer to be answered. But in that time, He began narrowing our vision to missions and children. Still, the possibilities seemed endless. So we continued to pray.

One night, I received a call from a woman I had never met. She proceeded to tell me that her sister and brother-in-law were missionaries in Guatemala. They happened to be home on furlough. This stranger thought I might like to hear their story. My curiosity was piqued, and I wondered how she had gotten my name. She told me her sister had given her a list of names to call. Now I was really curious!

"How did I get on this list?" I asked.

"You weren't on it," she said.

"Then how is it you're calling me?"

Her answer completely blew me away. She had called all the names on the list. Then the Lord spoke to her, directing her to the Christian Yellow Pages. When she opened the book, the first advertisement she saw was ours.

"I knew in my spirit that you and my sister had to meet," she said.

We had advertised in that publication only once, the year before. God had directed her not to a recent book but an old one.

When she told me they ran an orphanage for abused, abandoned, and neglected children in Guatemala, everything in my spirit leapt for joy! I knew beyond a shadow of a doubt this was the ministry the Lord himself had ordained for us to support.

When we met this missionary couple, our hearts were instantly joined, and we committed to a short-term missions' trip. Little did I know what God had in store. You see, on that first visit to Guatemala, another little one graced my path. It was the first of many trips to the "land of eternal springtime." Our newfound friends were the directors of an orphanage in a small village four hours from Guatemala City. At the time, their facility was experiencing some growing pains. There were more than seventy children living in the various homes the couple was renting, too many for their overcrowded rooms. What did they do? They cried out to God. Believing they already had more kids than they could handle, they made the painful decision that they couldn't take any more children. Their hearts were broken. But God!

The very next day, a young woman showed up at their doorstep with an eleven-month-old baby boy named Jose. He weighed a scant seven pounds. I had never seen a child so emaciated. His diet consisted of coffee. That's all.

I had seen how overwhelmed our friends were and asked if I could have the privilege of caring for little Jose until it was time for my family and me to return home. I can only imagine how frightened he was, away from his mommy, suddenly in the hands of a strange white woman who didn't even speak his language.

God, please help this baby know I'm safe; that I won't hurt him; that I will love him.

I held him close through the wee hours of that first

night, pacing the porch, praying with every breath that he wouldn't die in my arms. When he finally fell asleep, I laid him on my bed and snuggled close, listening to the gentle beat of his heart.

The sun rose bright and beautiful, and so did Jose! I knew it would be a long road to gain strength and health, but he had made it through the night. Praise God! Within days, Jose and I had become very attached to each other. When my family and I left Guatemala, it was as though I was leaving my own baby behind. Back in the States, my soul grieved for that little boy.

Jose grew strong and healthy under the loving care of our friends and their helpers. What a privilege it was to share in this miracle! I returned to Guatemala the next year, hoping he would remember me but realizing the chances were slim. Imagine my surprise when I stepped off the bus to the sweet sound of his voice shouting my name. He remembered me!

How gracious is our God! I had wounded one of His precious children years ago. But He loved me enough to forgive me and pour out His kindness on me in spite of myself. Why? So I could share it with others. He saw something in me that I had never seen in myself and gave me a second chance to get it right. He showed me that the smallest act of kindness truly is worth more than the greatest intention.

Time to Reflect

I think we can all remember times when we weren't as kind as we could have been. Your shortcomings in this area may not have been as blatant or hurtful as mine, but you know in your heart of hearts that you certainly could have done better. Or perhaps your unkindness has wounded someone terribly, and you're living with the guilt of that because you don't know how to fix it.

Whatever the case, you're not alone. As a matter of fact, unless you have absolutely no contact with the outside world, there's a good chance you've missed some opportunities. The Holy Spirit is in the business of giving us a holy nudge when someone in our corner of the world needs to know the love of Christ. Sadly, we're often too busy to hear His voice or too afraid to act on it.

Isn't it wonderful that God never gives up on us? Praise His name!

This exercise will give you a chance to examine where you rank on the kindness scale and open your eyes to the endless possibilities all around you.

Before you begin, take a moment to seek the Lord's guidance in this quest.

Father, I come before You now asking You to reveal

to me any situations where I've missed the mark in this area. My desire is to be an example of Your loving kindness to everyone around me, so they will be drawn to You. Please show me where I've fallen short. In Jesus's name. Amen.

Take a few moments to listen ... really listen before you move on.

By now, you probably have a picture or two in your mind when you were less than kind. Up until this point, you may have even thought you were justified in your actions. On a scale of 1–10, how do you feel?

Now that God has made you aware of situations you could have handled differently, it's time to get rid of the guilt that might be accompanying those memories. The Lord is waiting to forgive you. All you need to do is ask Him.

First John 1:9 reads, "But if we confess our sins to him, he is faithful and just to forgive us our sins and to cleanse us from all unrighteousness" (NKJV).

Lord, I am so very sorry for my actions. Please forgive me and help me to be a more kind, loving person. In Jesus's name. Amen.

Ah ... doesn't that feel better?

So what's next? It's time to move into phase two of this kindness challenge. This is the fun part! In this section, there will be a different assignment for each day of the week—a chance for you to perform a random act of kindness. Don't panic! These are not difficult tasks. Some may even seem to go totally unnoticed by everyone ... but God. Get ready to be blessed, dear one!

- Day one: Think of someone who's going through a tough time. Let them know (either by phone, text, or email) that you're praying for them. Then pray.
- Day two: Go to a department store and look for things that other shoppers have left in the wrong place. Then casually pick them up and put them in their proper place. You will be sure to bring a smile to the workers at the end of the day.
- Day three: Take a few Post-it notes and write the words, "Jesus loves you!" on them. Leave them in random places around town.
- Day four: Send a handwritten letter to a good friend instead of a text.
- Day five: Give a stranger a compliment.
- Day six: Visit a shut-in.
- Day seven: Go through your closet. If there are clothes you haven't worn in a year, donate them to charity.

These are merely suggestions. Please feel free to come up with your own ideas. You may even find you enjoy this so much you'll want to extend the week.

Instead, be kind to each other, tenderhearted,
forgiving one another, just as God
through Christ has forgiven you.
—Ephesians 4:32 NLT

Goodness

Be the reason someone feels loved and
believes in the goodness in people.

—Roy T. Bennett

I entered the unfamiliar classroom with a mixed bag
of emotions. September had always been my favorite
month on the school calendar. The excitement of
wrapping my arms around the little ones I'd missed
over the summer and welcoming frightened newcomers
with a smile and a hug filled me with joy. I loved
sharing fresh ideas with my coworkers and looked
forward to showering the three- and four-year-olds
under our care with all the love I stored in my heart
over the summer. But that was life in nursery school.
This September was a year of new beginnings, and I
found myself praying I'd made the right decision.

I was told very little about the elementary school

class I'd been assigned to. As a matter of fact, I hadn't even sought this job. Yet the interview panel thought I was the perfect candidate for what turned out to be the most challenging work environment of my career. During my interview, the principal made it very clear that there were many teacher's aide positions available, but they needed someone with my level of experience in the program for severely emotionally disturbed children. I should have foreseen the ride when told that it was the only full-time position available, and it came with full benefits.

Lord, is this really what You want for me?

There was no time to wait for His answer. School would be starting in a matter of weeks, and they needed a decision right then. For a split second, I thought, *I really want to take the easy road.* What came out of my mouth was, "I think God is calling me to work with disturbed children." Everyone on the interview panel was delighted and welcomed me aboard. They told me this was a special place for kindergarten through second graders who couldn't handle the typical classroom environment. They warned that I might hear some foul language out of the mouths of these little ones. That was it. No further explanation.

I spent the next few weeks trying to prepare myself for this adventure into the unknown. On the first day of school, I stood in front of the door of my classroom assignment with a sense of excitement mingled with anxiety.

God, help me be everything You're calling me to be.

Just then, the door of the classroom flew open, and I was greeted with a bright, smiling face.

"Oh, hi! You must be Gena, our new aide! We're so happy to have you here." She disappeared as quickly as she'd appeared, and I was left wondering what to do next. A quick survey of the room led me to believe this might not be so bad. After all, there were only eight students. How difficult could this be? But wait a minute! There were also four adults. Eight students, four adults. Uh-oh.

That first day was filled with episodes of anger and aggression, and I thought I'd made the biggest mistake of my life saying yes to this job. *How can this possibly be God's plan for me?* I went home that night exhausted and downhearted. I knew I shouldn't quit after the very first day, but that's exactly what I wanted to do.

God, what were You thinking? I'm the peace lover, remember? The pacifist. I don't know how to play tough guy. How in the world can I make a difference here? Please give me some kind of sign that I'm in the right place. I know I can do all things through Christ who strengthens me. So if this really is Your will, You'll give me all I need. I'm asking You to make it clear. A word or a song or something ...

Instantly, the words to a much-loved song from my childhood popped into my head. "Jesus loves the little children, all the children of the world. Red and yellow, black and white. They are precious in His sight. Jesus loves the little children of the world" (lyrics by George Frederick Root).

I fell to my knees and cried, "O God, forgive me. Help me to see these broken little children of Yours as You do. Use me as a channel of Your love."

It took some time to acclimate myself to this challenging, new world. I couldn't help wondering what had happened to these precious babies that made them so angry and violent. As the weeks stretched into months, I came to understand that many of our little boys had been victims of sexual abuse. My mind simply could not wrap around the horror of that. The oldest child in our class was only seven. How could anyone do such terrible things to them? My heart was broken, absolutely broken. Many were the nights I would lie awake thinking of them and praying for their safety. I had grown to love those little boys dearly, but I didn't see where I was making any kind of a difference. Each day, I would go home heavyhearted for them and angry at the perpetrators who created their brokenness.

"Lord, why have You placed me here? I'm not the right person. I'm just not the right person! I'm not strong enough. I can't take this," I cried into my pillow.

I desperately needed another sign from God, anything that would give me an out. But He was silent.

At the time, my husband, Gary, was actively involved in a Christian prison ministry. Each year, he and a team of nineteen men hosted a three-day event inside the prison walls. Over the course of the weekend, the inmates are given the opportunity to face their life choices head-on and discover the love and forgiveness Jesus Christ has to offer. I had heard the praise reports and believed wholeheartedly that people can and do change through the power of the Holy Spirit. However, the men in this prison were predominantly sex offenders. For all I knew, some could have been pedophiles. I understood Gary's passion for this ministry, but my mind could not get past the idea that those men were in prison for heinous crimes. They had done something unspeakable (possibly to a child), and I couldn't handle that. There I was working with the victims of such horror, while my husband was ministering to men who may have committed those very crimes. I was totally conflicted, wanting to support my husband on the one hand but harboring such unforgiveness toward the men he was serving on the other. I wanted nothing to do with them! Oh, I always made sure to pray. Yet my heart was far from pure in those moments. There was such anger in my soul toward them. Though I felt justified in my thinking, my attitude needed some adjusting. And deep inside, I knew it.

At one point, Gary was asked to serve as the leader for one of these weekends. I was so proud of him, but I knew exactly what that would mean. I would be expected to go to the closing service to support him. Part of me wanted nothing more than to be by his side. Nevertheless, my heart, so tainted by my opinion of the men behind those prison walls, made it difficult for me to drum up any real motivation.

The day of the service arrived, and I was no closer to having a right spirit than I had been months before. But Gary was counting on me. I simply had to go. At least the prison wasn't nearby. It would take an hour and a half to get there. Maybe, just maybe, God could help me with my attitude on the way. I had held onto those feelings for so long, though, I wondered if it would even be possible.

I hopped in the car, flipped the visor down, and took a long, hard look at myself in the mirror. The face staring back at me filled me with disgust. Judgment oozed out of every pore. *Lord, what has happened to me? This is not me.* I put on my best fake smile, but even that couldn't disguise my feelings. Flipping the visor up, I pulled out of the driveway, counting the hours until the day was but a memory.

Every moment of the trip was filled with anxious prayer.

How can I walk into that prison? The inmates can smell hypocrisy a mile away. Those men have spent the weekend with Gary. They see him as a good man, a godly man. They will expect his wife to be every bit as good and godly. O Lord, I don't want to be like this! Please help me see these men through Your eyes.

I arrived at the prison realizing my picture of that place was far removed from reality. I expected it to look like the county jail that I grew up near. Yes, there were bars on those windows. But that was the only indicator that it was a jail. This place, this prison, looked like something out of a movie. Fifteen-foot-high fencing surrounded the compound. Double rows of razor wire enveloped both the bottom and the top of the fence. Just pulling into the parking lot filled my already unsettled mind with raw fear. My heart raced wildly, and it was all I could do to get out of the car. I wasn't sure my shaking knees would support me. *God, You're going to have to be my legs. I can't do this otherwise.*

Somehow, I managed to cross the parking lot to the building referred to as the sally port, the place Gary had instructed me to go to. How relieved I was to see some people I knew arriving for the service! But my attitude toward the prisoners I would soon be face-to-face with hadn't changed.

As frightened as I was going through security and hearing that heavy metal door slam behind me, a peace began to penetrate my unsettled soul. The Holy Spirit was indeed at work.

The service itself moved me to tears as each man's testimony spoke so powerfully of the forgiveness offered to each of us through Jesus Christ when we come to Him with repentant hearts. I listened with rapt attention, wanting to believe that each was speaking totally sincere words. The knowledge that those behind bars can be master manipulators somehow slipped my mind. Even knowing that these types of crimes have the highest rate of recidivism didn't seem to affect me the same way. Was my naivete showing? Probably. Was God changing my heart just as I had asked Him to? Most definitely! In the moments that followed, I started to see those men not just as criminals who had perpetrated horrific crimes but as part of my assignment from God. They needed Jesus, and He was calling me to make a difference in their lives.

Suddenly, my prayers on their behalf were filled with urgency and passion. I started seeing them through God's eyes of love. As I wholeheartedly embraced this new way of thinking, the Lord gave me a platform I never would have sought or expected.

One of the prison chaplains discovered that our family traveled in music ministry together and asked Gary if we would consider holding a concert in the prison. In the past, I would have responded with something like, "Oh, no ... not my thing." But the

Lord had worked such a change in my heart that I jumped at the chance. Little did I know He would birth a message in me that He wanted the men to hear.

The night of that first concert arrived, and though God had softened my attitude toward the men, there was still a twinge of leftover apprehension hanging onto me. *God, I know You've given me a message to speak. Give me the confidence and boldness I need to deliver it.* I no sooner finished praying when the peace of God fell on me. I choked back my misgiving and walked into that prison ready to be God's mouthpiece.

We entered the auditorium, fully expecting to get right to work setting up our equipment, but God had other plans. We were warmly greeted by a group of inmates who were known as the prayer team. I had no idea such a thing even existed. These men had been given special permission to come to the concert early to pray over us. What an amazing gift! We stood in a circle and felt the power of the Holy Spirit in such a tangible way with each prayer that was lifted on our behalf. From that moment on, I was able to stand unafraid and boldly proclaim the word God had birthed in me.

The Lord has called us back to that prison many times, but I will never forget that first concert—the night God helped me "do it afraid," as Joyce Meyer would say, and be the reason others would feel loved and believe in the goodness in people.

Time to Reflect

Let's begin this session by asking ourselves a simple question: "Who am I?" Think about it. Your thoughts may have automatically turned to your occupation. But that really doesn't answer the question, does it? All that tells the world is what you do for a living. It says nothing of who you are. Your career doesn't define you.

Perhaps you wear many hats at this point in your life. So your answer might be all-encompassing. You might think of your family obligations first. You see yourself as a wife, a dad, a grandma, or a caretaker. Maybe your involvements in the community take center stage in your mind. You're a Sunday school teacher, a baseball coach, or an advocate to stop human trafficking. And those things would speak accurately of what you do with your time. But that still doesn't answer the question.

This next step might be difficult at best, but it's an important one nonetheless. Stand in front of your favorite mirror and take a long, hard look at yourself. Make sure it's your favorite mirror. You know the one I'm talking about. Who do you see?

All too often, we sell ourselves short, believing

the lie that we're not as good as others for one reason or another. We're not as good-looking, as smart, as thin, or as put together as our neighbor next door. We fall into the trap that our ugly past has somehow tarnished our future as well. We long to be people of great faith like those who've gone before us. Yet our overly committed lives keep us from being all we've convinced ourselves God wants us to be.

For some of us, that door swings the other way. We know the beauty we possess on the outside and compare ourselves to others based on that alone. But on the inside, the place no one sees ...

Take a look in that mirror again. Who are you? Are you the reason others believe in the goodness of people? Think about it.

Oh, my friends, life is short, whether we're talking about life expectancy or end-time prophecy. Let's not waste it comparing ourselves to anyone else. All God is really looking for is a willing vessel to represent Him, flawed and imperfect as we may be. Yet as much as He loves us just as we are, rest assured He always has more for us. Isn't that wonderful? Our job is to be willing to face the truth about ourselves as He reveals it to us, allowing Him to change us from the inside out. Then and only then can we experience the joy of spreading His goodness to a hurting world.

In the same way, let your light shine before
others, that they may see your good deeds
and glorify your Father in Heaven.
—Matthew 5:16 NIV

Gracious Lord, I know there have been times when
I've misjudged people based on nothing more than
appearance. O God, You know my heart. I long to be
the reason others believe in the goodness of people.
I know that the fruit of true goodness comes only
from You. Your Word tells me to "stop judging by
mere appearances" (John 7:24 NIV). Thank You for
revealing to me where I fall short in this area. Help me
to rise above my shortcomings and be Your light in all
the corners of my world.

Faithfulness

God is faithful even when his children are not.

—Max Lucado

I've heard it said there are few things on earth more faithful than a dog. After all, who else would sit by the door all day long, awaiting your return? Not many humans, that's for sure.

When my beloved aunt Gena was but a child, she longed for a dog like that. You know, the kind that never leaves your side unless absolutely necessary. The kind that practically leaps out of his skin with excitement every time he sees you. The kind that puts you first above all else. Many of the kids in her neighborhood were blessed with dogs that would wait for them at the school bus stop. Day after day, Aunt Gena would watch the children's furry friends greet their owners with tails wagging and sloppy, wet kisses.

Holding back her tears, she secretly wished she could experience that. Unfortunately, not everyone in the family shared her passion, and a "no pets allowed" rule was strictly enforced.

Several years passed without a pet pooch to love. When she had just about given up hope, the most *interesting* thing happened. Now, wouldn't it be a lovely ending to this story if I told you the perfect dog miraculously appeared at her door, with the entire family falling instantly in love with him? What actually happened, however, is far more amusing.

It was a sunny day, making it difficult to see clearly out the school bus windows. As the bus neared her stop, she thought she spotted something unusual amid all the canine companions.

"Please tell me that's not what I think it is," she whispered under her breath.

But as the bus coasted to a stop, her worst fears were realized. It was a chicken—one of her family's chickens! It had followed all the dogs and was waiting patiently for her arrival.

"This cannot be happening," she said.

Those words no sooner left her lips when the entire bus full of children started laughing hysterically … at her! Being the brunt of many a joke throughout her life, she had no doubt this would only add fuel to the fire. Now she had a big ol' Rhode Island Red meeting her at the bus stop! Do you know that bird faithfully walked to the bus stop with the other pets every single day after that? It didn't matter what Aunt Gena said to it. It didn't even matter when she totally ignored it. That chicken remained faithful, *no matter what!*

Oh, how I wish the same could be said for us humans! Don't you? Most of us tend to think of ourselves as faithful, though our definition of that word might be slightly skewed. As long as we haven't engaged in an extramarital affair, then we qualify— we are somehow better than those who have. Well, guess again, my friends.

Every single characteristic listed in the fruit of the Spirit passage in Galatians 5 is an attribute of God, which we should be striving to display as Christ's representatives. Obviously, God has never had an extramarital affair. Then how did He demonstrate faithfulness? By keeping His promises. Need some proof? Check this out:

1. He saved Noah and family from destruction, and humanity was preserved as a result—just as He promised (Genesis 6:9–9:17 NIV).
2. He gave once-childless hundred-year-old Abraham countless descendants—just as He promised (Genesis 17 NIV).
3. He restored the nation of Israel (1948)—just as He promised (Ezekiel 11:17 NIV).

4. But the greatest of all is that He sent His son Jesus (Matthew 1:21–22 NIV), and through Him we have everlasting life—just as He promised (John 3:16 NIV).

We are certainly not God, nor does He expect us to be. But we should always be learning from His example as well as from our own mistakes. They say most people do the best they can with what they know at the time. I believe there's an element of truth in that. If I could travel back in time with what I know now, my young adulthood would look far different. Did I do the best I could with what I knew at the time, though? I can't honestly say that I did.

In the early days of my newfound faith, I really didn't know what it meant to be a Christian. Since people at the church were inviting me to be a part of many different ministries, I thought that was how it was supposed to be. You accepted Christ, then said yes to whatever any church person asked you to do.

Choir? Great! I love to sing! Vacation Bible school? Awesome! Kids are my thing! Join Bible study? Well, I couldn't very well say no to that one, could I? Parsonage Committee? Why not? I don't know a lot about decorating, but it sounds like fun. Staff-Parish Relations Committee? I've always been a peacemaker. That would be a good fit. Junior choir director? Oh, yeah! I would love that! Elementary youth director?

Hmmm … my kids are in that age group. I should do that. Church secretary? That was once my career path. How perfect! And the list went on and on and on.

It never occurred to me at the time that my primary ministry was at home. After all, my husband wasn't walking with the Lord, and our children needed a good example of what a Christian was supposed to look like, right?

Trying to balance my boys' activities, all my church involvements, keeping up with our house, and working from home was next to impossible. I was spreading myself too thin, and I didn't know it.

My husband grew more impatient by the day as I was running off to meetings several evenings a week—many times leaving him home with the children after his long day at work. My new lifestyle certainly didn't help his anger issues.

If he would just become a Christian, he would understand, I would reason.

No one told me my priorities were mixed up. No one offered any suggestions. No one even spoke to me about the fact that I was trying to do too much. But then again, I had become quite proficient at hiding the truth. How would they have known? It wasn't until a debilitating illness struck my body that I had no choice but to slow down. The long months of testing and recuperation gave me ample time to consider what I had been doing to myself and my family. Some changes were in order. I just couldn't figure out what that was supposed to look like. All I knew was that God had the answer. So I prayed ... and I prayed ... and I prayed. Yet He was silent.

Admitting my weakness was a very humbling experience. All those feelings of insecurity came flooding back to me. *I thought I was good enough, but I'm still not. Maybe I never will be.*

I had to cut back on my crazy schedule. There was no choice in the matter. I couldn't keep up. For the longest time, it didn't occur to me that the busyness of my life had caused the illness. Until I was stricken with it, however, the thought that I was not being faithful to my family never crossed my mind either. I thought putting the Lord first meant doing everything possible for the church. How I wish someone had told me where my family was in God's list of priorities.

It wasn't until I asked the Lord to show me how to live my life His way that things started to change. Different ministries that didn't consume all my time began to emerge. That was just the tip of the iceberg. The best was yet to come.

After fourteen years of praying and waiting, my husband finally accepted Christ as his Savior! In an instant, everything changed. God totally delivered him from his anger! He stopped punching holes in the walls, there was no more yelling, and the lawn mower (often seen flying across the garage) became his friend. He even started smiling! My heart was exploding with thankfulness and joy. *I wonder what God will do with him, with us now.*

It wasn't long before the Lord launched us into a traveling music ministry, one we are still involved in today.

But wait ... there's more!

Prior to my illness, I had been struggling to find quiet time for prayer and communion with God in my busy day. Try as I might, it just wasn't happening. No matter what I did, there was always some kind of roadblock. The only moments that weren't filled with something were those seconds just before drifting off to sleep. Unfortunately, my body was usually so exhausted by then that prayer wasn't even on my radar. But one night, there was too much on my mind, and sleep just wouldn't come. So I poured my heart out to the Lord. And then I waited ... and waited ... and waited. Nothing. Just as I was about to doze off, God showed up, though I didn't recognize Him in that moment. A picture of myself speaking before a large group of people flashed through my brain. Startled, I sat straight up in bed.

"What just happened? Was that a vision or something? God, if that's You, then You need to know something. I don't have the wisdom. I don't have the knowledge. I don't know how to make that happen. I don't know what to do, and I don't even want to know. I'm not doing it!" I muttered with authority.

So I kept my word and did nothing about it. Nor did I tell a soul … for twenty-five years! Occasionally, the memory of that vision would intrude on my thoughts for but a moment. Each time, I would literally shake my head and dismiss the idea as quickly as it had entered my brain.

After my husband accepted Christ, the Lord began a work in me as well. As much as I had always loved my family, it took Gary's conversion to make me see how very important my role was in all their lives. God had handpicked me to be a wife and a mother. Running off to meetings many nights of the week wasn't nearly as appealing anymore.

Lord, please help me prioritize my life. Show me what I'm called to do.

It all began with a women's ministry. Overnight, I became a teacher, a speaker, a counselor … a leader. And I loved it! But God was far from finished with me.

I had spent months planning a special evening for these women who had become my friends. My heart's desire was for them to rise up and become the women of God they were called to be; women after His own heart; women of great faith.

I arrived at the church to set up hours early, making sure there was ample time for me to engage in prayer in the sanctuary as well. After putting on the finishing touches in the fellowship hall, I glanced at my watch.

Yes! I still have over an hour.

I headed to the sanctuary, excited to have the opportunity to meet with God alone in that holy place on behalf of the women who were coming to the event. It just never occurred to me that the Lord was about to birth something new in me.

After praying over each pew and believing in a mighty move of the Holy Spirit, everything was ready. Yet when I turned to leave, it was as if there was cement in my shoes. I couldn't make myself walk out the door. Not knowing what else to do, I did what came naturally for me and began to praise God in song. Just as I lifted my hands, the vision that God had birthed in me all those years ago came flooding back. Only this time, twenty-five years later, I didn't resist. I knew in my spirit it was time.

Seriously, Lord? Why me? I'm no one special. How can I, flawed as I am, make that kind of difference?

Immediately, all the old doubts and fears came crashing in like a flood.

What if that wasn't God? I'll never be able to do this, and I'll look like a fool.

So I did the only thing I could think of at the time. I asked God to prove it … three ways. My reasoning? It would take years to receive those answers. That would give me ample time to adjust to the idea … or not. I vowed to tell no one, not even my husband, until I was absolutely certain.

My first confirmation came two days later. Two days! It was Sunday morning. After the service, our pastor approached me, pointed his finger at me, and said, "You need to stop running from God. There's a call on your life, and you're not answering it."

Whoa! I thought.

I smiled, turned away, and muttered under my breath, "I wonder if that's number one."

The very next Sunday, another devout man of God pulled me aside and with all sincerity said, "You need to stop running from God. There's a call on your life, and you're not answering it."

This can't be happening. Could this be number two already?

A few days later, a publication arrived in the mail that I had not sent for. Yet it was addressed to me. It's title? *Higher Education, Christian Colleges.* I couldn't deny God's call any longer. In less than two weeks, He had confirmed it three ways, just as I had asked. He is so faithful!

Before I did anything else, I knew it was time to speak to my husband. But how would he respond? I wanted to believe he would be supportive, yet experience told me not to expect it.

"God, please speak to Gary's heart before I ever utter a word. Let him know this idea really is from You."

When I knew I couldn't put it off any longer, I waited for what I thought would be just the right time to talk to him. Shaking in my boots, I sat down next to him and told him everything that had happened, from my first vision to my last confirmation. His reply totally shocked me. He looked me square in the eye, smiled, and said, "Honey, it's about time."

I could hardly believe my ears! He knew all along! Thus began my journey into pastoral ministry, with the support of not just my husband but our boys as well.

You would think that trying to find the time to study would have been impossible with a young family. Nevertheless, God made a way. I never missed a ball game or a concert, kept up with the housework, and spent quality time with my husband and each of the kids.

Though I never would have sought credentials, having them has given credibility to my words. Over the years, the Lord has continued to open doors for many speaking opportunities. Who would have guessed?

God once again proved Himself faithful, in spite of the times when I was anything but that.

Time to Reflect

What's the first thing that comes to mind when you hear the word *faithfulness*? Do your thoughts automatically turn to your spouse or significant other? Maybe you are more likely to think of your dog. Or better yet, your pet chicken. Your brain might have even conjured up someone who has no connection with you at all—a celebrity, someone who made the ten o'clock news perhaps. In that case, the word that more accurately describes your thoughts would probably be unfaithfulness, wouldn't it?

If you're anything like most of the world, your focus was not on yourself, was it? It's true. God is faithful, even when his children are not. Isn't that amazing? In this session, you will have the opportunity to examine your own faithfulness.

Let's start with a few questions, shall we? Take a moment to honestly consider each one.

- How would you define the word faithful?
- Does that word describe you?
- Do those around you consider you faithful?
- How do you feel about that?

- Have you been faithful to the people in your circle? Think about it.
- How about God? Have you been faithful to Him?

Lamentations 3:22–23 reads, "The faithful love of the Lord never ends! His mercies never cease. Great is his faithfulness; His mercies begin afresh each morning" (NLT).

So what does that mean? Simply put, in spite of our sins, our mistakes, our bloopers and blunders, He is faithful to forgive. He has every reason to punish us, but He chooses to shower us with mercy. There may still be consequences to our actions, but we can rest assured that God will always be faithful to forgive when we come to Him with a repentant heart. Oh, my friend, isn't it wonderful to know His mercies are new every morning? How can we ever repay Him?

The answer is quite simple. We follow the instructions. We pray (Romans 12:12 NLT). We read and obey His Word (John 8:31–32; 2 John 1:6 NLT). We choose to separate ourselves from the things of the world that are ungodly (2 Cor. 6:17 NLT).

How about you? Are you ready to begin your journey in faithfulness? I can promise you won't regret it.

Dear God, I am in awe of Your faithfulness. Even in the times when I disappoint You the most, You remain faithful. Your mercies truly are new every morning. I know I don't deserve that blessing. But I'm so very thankful for it. I come before You today asking Your forgiveness for the times I've not been faithful to You or the people in my corner of the world. The very thought of those things cuts to the core of my being. Please, Lord, help me to be more like You. Thank You for Your faithful, forgiving, merciful heart. I love You, my Lord and my God.

8

Gentleness

I choose gentleness … Nothing is won by force.
—Max Lucado

Talk to most anyone after their first missions' trip, and they'll tell you they left a big part of their heart there. Many are changed in ways they find hard to describe. Some quickly make plans to return. Others feel called by God to serve in full-time ministry there. Me? Well, I would say all the above applied. Not that everything I thought was true or right, but Guatemala was where my heart longed to be.

The night before our departure from that beautiful country, it was all I could do to hold myself together. Based on nothing more than feelings, my assumption was that God wanted us to stay. Yet we were leaving.

Why do we have to leave? Why can't we just stay here? Why would God call us to this amazing place where there's so much need just to send us back to our own spoiled country?

None of it made sense to my breaking heart.

Saying goodbye to the children and my new friends was every bit as excruciating as I'd imagined it would be. I held baby Jose in my arms, gazing into his beautiful face, wondering if I'd ever see him again. Ten days just wasn't enough time. Tears fell like rain. I couldn't imagine life without this little one.

I'd like to say the flight home was uneventful, but that would be a lie. Right there on that plane, a change began in me. One that I didn't see coming. One that almost destroyed me. Guatemala had become home to me. Leaving there felt wrong in every way. Thoughts of leaving the land I had come to love consumed me.

They say there's tremendous healing in allowing yourself the freedom to cry. For me, it wasn't a matter of surrendering to the pain though. I couldn't have stopped the tears if I tried. As we flew into the Houston airport, something horrible rose up in me— an anger I had never dealt with in my life. Gazing out the window, there were swimming pools as far as the eye could see. Maybe I hadn't noticed them on the way to Guatemala. I can't say for sure. Yet in that moment, it was as if I was seeing them for the very first time.

Are you kidding me? How could this be? Look at all those spoiled, rich people. Don't they know there are children living in the city dump and dying of starvation in Guatemala?

By the time we landed, I had convinced myself that we lived not just in the land of plenty but the land of greed—that there were no truly humble, caring people left in the good ol' USA. A sense of guilt washed over me in the process of unpacking. Not wanting to be associated with either that lifestyle or the attitude I thought accompanied it, I first set about ridding myself of anything that would make me appear selfish. Five garbage bags later, my closet contained only what was necessary for everyday living. Everything else was donated to a local charity. You would have thought that drastic action would be enough to set my mind at ease. Yet it wasn't. A guilty conscience still disrupted my days.

Was that of God? Of course not! Those nagging ideas continued to discolor my world though, and the thought occurred to me that God was trying to raise me up to bring awareness to this selfish culture. It suddenly became my duty to save everyone from this plight before it was too late.

In my mind, I had a platform. After all, I was a women's ministry leader. Why not use that for the good of others? My words, my actions, everything about me, however, screamed anger, not love. My witness was anything but Godly, which was damaging my reputation and any hope of raising funds for the orphanage in Guatemala. Yet I was totally oblivious to what was happening.

I thought of myself as a modern-day Mahatma Gandhi, a champion for the poor. In my zeal, all I was doing was trying to force anyone and everyone to jump on board with me and save all the starving, abused children in Guatemala. I wasn't even aware that the way I presented my passion for the ministry was turning people off.

My own family became targets of my obsession. In addition to giving away half my belongings, I started to believe that God was asking us to move there. He never once spoke that word to me, mind you. I conjured that one up all by myself. I even began praying that the Lord would speak to my husband's stubborn heart so he would see I was right.

After six months of unsuccessful attempts to change the minds and hearts of those in my corner of the world, a dear friend spoke the hard truth I needed to hear. She said, "Gena, you need to stop this! You're blaming everyone in America for the fact that people are starving over three thousand miles away. Guess what, honey. You're an American! And this is not our fault." My mouth dropped open, tears filled my eyes, and I stood dumbstruck. *How could she say that to me? I'm only trying to help.*

She gave me a few moments to collect myself and let her words, her heartfelt words, settle into my soul.

In those brief seconds, the conviction of the Holy Spirit resonated in my spirit.

"You're right," I said. "I had no idea. I really didn't."

As I bowed in humble repentance, the Lord showered me with His mercy and love. From then on, when I spoke of Guatemala, it was with a very different voice—one filled with compassion and love, as God would have it.

Four years and four trips later, Guatemala became my home away from home. Gone was the longing to live there permanently. No more tears boarding the plane for America. No more prayers for things to be different. Just a thankful heart for the opportunity to make a difference in a part of the world I never would have dreamed I'd visit. Yes, part of my heart will always be in that country, but I had seen the error of my ways and allowed the Lord to use that for His glory and my good.

However, we are all a work in progress, are we not? It took some time after my Guatemalan attitude adjustment to fully understand that every person is not called by God to be involved in every ministry. When my husband would speak of the men he worked with behind prison walls, a big part of me was always thankful there were people called to that. But there was nothing driving me to participate in that kind of ministry.

When missionaries would speak at our church, my heart would be broken … for the moment. I would feel led to give an offering and even commit to pray for them. Yet unless God clearly spoke to my heart to get involved in another way, that's where it would end.

You're probably wondering at this point where the problem was, right? After all, scripture makes it plain that we are all gifted in one way or another, each one called specifically by the Lord. "There are different kinds of spiritual gifts, but the same Spirit is the source of them all. There are different kinds of service, but we serve the same Lord. God works in different ways, but it is the same God who does the work in all of us" (1 Cor. 12:4–6 NLT).

The issue was my guilty conscience every time I said no. It took an act of God for me to come to grips with that.

The term human trafficking had come to the forefront in the eighties as protests to raise awareness about the exploitation of women and children were popping up across the country. From the moment I first heard how widespread this atrocity was, it struck a chord in me. *What difference can one person make though?* I wondered. In my spirit, I knew God was calling me to pray. Yet in my heart, that wasn't enough. Over the years, the plight of these innocent victims would come to mind, and it would rock my world for a time. I would pray more fervently and ask God to show me how I could effect change. It was thirty years later that an opportunity presented itself. Our church started an anti–human trafficking group. The idea was to raise awareness in our community. Sounds like a perfect fit, doesn't it? Little did I know it wasn't my calling.

In the beginning, there were prayer meetings, trainings, and outreach events—all of which I attended. But something was wrong. Though my passion for the plight of those being exploited never waned, there was no peace in my soul about my involvement in this ministry. My mouth started to get in the way again as I tried to cover my insecurities. I became more vocal and almost forceful (notice I said "almost") in my approach as I tried to convince others of their need to get involved.

I went through the motions, trying to make myself believe I was in the right place, exactly where God had chosen for me to be. A steel-plated marshmallow. That was me. Tough girl on the outside but a pile of mush on the inside. Try as I might, I could not seem to muster the courage and strength the other women in the group seemed to possess. Even sitting through a movie about this topic was next to impossible without having to run from the room, physically ill, hoping to make it to the bathroom before I got sick. The list of excuses for my behavior grew with each incident.

Having convinced myself this was merely confirmation of my passion for the ministry, I was certain if I could just get enough people to join the fight, my confidence would grow and my anxiety would disappear … like magic. Though I wasn't as forceful in my approach as I'd been in my post-Guatemala days, others probably wouldn't have described me as gentle either.

It wasn't until we embarked on our first hotel outreach that God really broke through to me. Our job? To raise awareness. We traveled in packs of four—two were to be the spokespeople, while the other two remained in the vehicle, keeping watch *with the car running* in case a quick escape was necessary. I was absolutely terrified! Everything went as planned, thankfully without incident. But my anxious soul could not seem to rest.

That night, lying in bed, alone with my thoughts, I poured my heart out to God.

Lord, what is wrong here? I can't seem to settle into this. I have no peace. I'm still shaken when nothing frightening or out of the ordinary even happened today. Why am I like this? No one else even seems concerned, and I'm scared to death. Please show me how to fix this.

Instantly, a scripture reference popped into my head, Genesis 16:1–3. Not knowing what that passage was, I grabbed my Bible and a flashlight and pulled the covers over my head in hopes of not waking my husband as I began to read: "Now Sarai, Abram's wife, had not been able to bear children for him. But she had an Egyptian servant named Hagar. So Sarai said to Abram, 'The LORD has prevented me from having children. Go and sleep with my servant. Perhaps I can have children through her.' And Abram agreed with Sarai's proposal. So Sarai, Abram's wife, took Hagar the Egyptian servant and gave her to Abram as a wife. (This happened ten years after Abram had settled in the land of Canaan)" (NLT).

Hmmm ... what does that have to do with me? Oh, I get it! They were told to wait—just wait. They chose to act when God never called them to do that. That's it! God called me to pray, but I tried to force so much more.

In those moments, I learned the true meaning of gentleness. It has nothing to do with weakness, and it means so much more than simply being polite. It's having a humble spirit; one that listens to the voice of God and acts accordingly; one that does not voice their opinion out of anger; one that restrains their behavior with others; one that can speak the truth in love, as Christ did.

It's been an interesting journey, this lesson in gentleness. Many ministries have drifted in and out of my life since then, each one capturing me for a season. But as impassioned as I've found myself at the time, I've never once reverted back to that type of forceful attitude that consumed me for a while. Just as Max Lucado stated, I, too, choose gentleness because nothing is won by force.

Time to Reflect

Picture a newborn puppy. We all know how very fragile they are, don't we? So we treat them with tender loving care. But what if that puppy grows up to be a challenge? What then?

Think for a moment about the people in your sphere of influence. How easy it is to speak gently to someone who's like-minded! What about those who disagree with you though? Where are you on the gentleness scale then?

It should be the norm to treat ourselves with a measure of gentleness as well. And for some, that's as natural as breathing. For others, however, it's far more difficult.

Yet God calls us to be gentle. "Pursue righteousness and a godly life, along with faith, love, perseverance, and gentleness" (1 Timothy 6:11b NLT).

In this session, you will take the first step toward maintaining a gentle spirit. Try this on for size:

1. List the folks who challenge this characteristic in you the most. Maybe it's your spouse, your children, an employee, or a friend. Is there

someone who gets on your last nerve? Perhaps the person you are least gentle with is yourself.

2. Next to each name, write down why it's difficult for you to be gentle with them. Take your time with this part.

3. Now ask the Father to bless each of them. If you're on the list, that includes you. No, it's not wrong to seek God's blessings for yourself. The idea is not to focus on the things you could do on your own. What you're really asking for is what the Lord and only the Lord has the power to give you. Nothing else.

4. Now ask the Father to help you see the people on your list as He sees them.

5. Make this your daily practice. I think you'll be pleasantly surprised to watch the list get shorter and shorter as you begin to look at these people differently.

Oh, my friends, life is short, whether you're talking about end-time prophecy or life expectancy. Let's not waste another moment of it. God loves you so much. All He is really looking for is a willing vessel to represent Him—not perfect, just willing.

O God, how very patient You are! I know Your desire is for me to not slander anyone and avoid quarreling.

Instead, I should be gentle and show true humility to everyone (Titus 3:2 NLT). Yet there are times I've fallen short in each of those areas. In those moments when I'm tempted to be anything but gentle, remind me who I represent as a follower of Christ. Help me to temper my words with love.

9

Self-Control

Self-control is knowing you can
but deciding you won't.
—Dr. Bob Gray Sr.

"Betcha can't eat just one." Lays potato chips first launched their famous slogan in the early 1960s. It quickly became a part of their most successful ad campaign ever. With the help of celebrity endorsements, the chips reached international claim to fame as well. Why did it work? Because it seemed to be true. Once you opened that bag, its entire contents were gone before you knew what happened. That slogan proved to be great for their business but certainly taxed the restraint of its consumers. I know I could never eat just one. Could you?

Self-control. That's the name of the game. It sounds good on paper, but oh, how hard it is to live out! Never was my sense of restraint put to the test to a greater extent than during the time I lovingly refer to as baby adulthood.

Ah, college days—that carefree time when you think you're indestructible, that the world is your oyster, and at the ripe old age of eighteen, you know everything there is to know about life. It took me a while to come to the realization that being on the dean's list didn't necessarily mean I was blessed with common sense. However, anyone who knew me back then was well aware of that obvious lack in my personality.

Always the prankster, I became known as the queen of practical jokes. Whatever my creative little mind concocted, I acted on. I was the life of the party. And I loved it. I'd found my niche. I was finally good enough. Over time, my friends learned to be on high alert, always expecting the unexpected from me. They all knew that if they let their guard down for even one second, I would be up to something. It was not at all unusual for any one of them to find their bed short-sheeted, toothpaste on the earpiece of the phone, a favorite shoe among the missing, their towel or clothes mysteriously disappearing while they showered, and so on. Each crazy stunt would bring gales of laughter, feeding my already out-of-control behavior. I rarely thought about the possible consequences before I did anything. In my infinite wisdom, I actually thought I could talk my way out of any trouble that might occur as a result of my stupidity, that no one would ever get hurt. After all, it was all in fun. No harm done, right? Wrong!

Halloween was right around the corner. My girlfriends and I had gathered to carve pumpkins on a lazy Sunday afternoon. I came up with what seemed like the ultimate gag and could hardly wait to see how it would play out. While we were scraping the stringy, gooey mess out of our pumpkins, I announced to our little group that I had heard some fascinating information about pumpkin guts. Scientists had discovered that using that slimy stuff for a facial was found to be very successful at clearing up acne. I dug away at my pumpkin, nonchalantly glancing from one face to the next to see if anyone bought into my outlandish claims. Some of the girls paid little to no attention to my words, while others snickered to themselves. In all likelihood, they had gotten so used to my nonsense they figured I was making it all up anyway.

Just as I was about to give in and tell them the truth, one brave girl in our circle of friends decided to give it a try. Everyone else was hard at work, barely looking up from their masterpieces.

I, however, thoroughly enjoyed watching my suitemate spread that icky mess all over her face. You'd think that would have been enough to satisfy my comedic personality, wouldn't you? But no. I had to carry it one step further. I told her that for it to be effective, she needed to leave it on for at least twenty minutes. *Twenty minutes!* Much to my amazement, she didn't even bat an eye. So I set the timer and waited.

The clock ticked away ever so slowly as I waited to spring the surprise on her—that this was just another one of my little jokes. I was sure she would see it as nothing more than a brilliant prank. We'd get a kick out of it, and that would be the end of it. Had I known the consequence, I never would have concocted this crazy scheme.

The timer went off. I watched intently as she began to wash the chunks of pumpkin and seeds off her face. It took but one look at her complexion to realize I'd made a gross error in judgment. Though her skin was indeed very soft, the pumpkin had stained her face the most horrific shade of orange. I was absolutely mortified!

Dropping to my knees in horror, I burst into tears. My know-it-all, anything-for-a-joke attitude had wounded someone I really cared about, and I couldn't fix it.

Then my dear friend did the unimaginable. She reached down, helped me to my feet, looked into my tear-filled eyes, and with the most loving smile said, "It's okay, Gena. I forgive you. I know you would never do anything to hurt me on purpose."

Yes, it was a lesson in unconditional love. Yes, it was a lesson in the true meaning of forgiveness. It was also a jolt into reality. That piece of paper signed by the dean of students told the world I was smart. But it was a redheaded little angel who made me realize I didn't know it all. I was intelligent all right, but I had a lot to learn in the school of wisdom.

Looking back, that experience should have given me cause to realize I had a problem with self-control. Unfortunately, that's not the case. Oh, I felt terribly guilty over what I had done to my friend. That's as far as it went though.

From that point on, I still used my creative brain to prank my friends. I still drank like a fish, spent my parents' money like it was water, and did basically anything I wanted to do, giving no regard to the consequences of my actions. After all, I was young and invincible. What could possibly happen? Little did I know I was setting the stage for the rest of my life.

Neither graduation, marriage, nor even children managed to change this imbalance in my world. I simply transferred my extremes from pranking, drinking, and overspending to overeating. While my husband was at work, I would binge all day on whatever was in the house. Though it wasn't referred to as stress eating back then, that's exactly what it was. After a few days of that, a weigh-in would be in order. If I had gained as much as a pound, overexercising and starving myself became the solution. My weight fluctuated with every extreme.

Things took a marked turn for the worse when I began teaching high-impact aerobics at our church. With no set program to go by, creating routines required a strenuous four- to five-hour daily workout. It was incredibly hard on my body, but I had a goal. I had always worn a size twelve, and I wanted desperately to be thin enough to wear a seven. When the weight wasn't falling off as quickly as I wanted, I decided to change my diet ... drastically. I ate next to nothing for months and finally reached my goal. At 5'6", I weighed a scant 107 pounds. When I looked in the mirror, though, I never saw a skinny girl. The image staring back at me was still fat, and I hated that. Friends and family tried to convince me I was too thin, but I wouldn't listen. Instead, I stayed on the same destructive path and hoped for better results. Of course, that didn't happen.

Some months later, I woke up one morning extremely sick to my stomach. I thought I'd picked up some kind of bug and that I would feel like my old self in a day or two. But each passing week found me sicker and weaker. Multiple trips to the doctor and tests galore proved nothing. In one short month, I had lost twenty-five pounds, and no one could figure out why. Having no other answer, the medical professionals were convinced I was expecting a baby.

I knew I wasn't, but they wouldn't listen to me. Eight negative pregnancy tests later, they finally gave up on that diagnosis.

What's wrong with me? Why can't they figure this out?

At the time, my husband, Gary, and I were on the two-child plan, which we had already happily achieved. Interestingly enough, after the eighth pregnancy test came back negative, I found myself feeling disappointed. With my heart strangely saddened, speaking with Gary was all I could think of. But how would he react? After all, the plan was working. Besides that, I was still terribly sick with no resolution in sight. The thought of having another little one in our home consumed my thoughts though. I simply had to talk to him.

Knowing timing was everything, I waited for the perfect moment to break the news. The children had gone to bed. The house was quiet. Even the dog was asleep. Gary was in a good mood, having had a decent day at work. This was it. I took a deep breath and approached him with as much sweetness as I could muster and poured my heart out. I expected him to put his foot down, reminding me of our plan. Imagine my surprise to discover we were on the same page. He'd been thinking about having another baby all along. I could not have been happier!

History repeated itself, and I conceived quickly.

Though doctors had come up with neither a diagnosis nor a solution, my sickness mysteriously disappeared. No nausea, no morning sickness ... nothing. For the first time in months, I felt well. As a matter of fact, I wasn't sick a day of the pregnancy. It was as if God was saying, "Honey, I've got this amazing blessing just waiting for you, but you've got to get off the two-child plan."

Our third son, Chris, was born on a frigid day in January. I never could have foreseen the joy that child would bring into our lives. Gifted with a beautiful singing voice, he became our ministry partner before his eleventh birthday. For years, Gary and I had been traveling throughout New York and Pennsylvania, proclaiming the love of God through song and the spoken word. At a very young age, our son began performing a solo number at each service. Everywhere we ministered, folks were in awe of his gift. Little did we know, there was talent we were yet to discover.

Gary and I often found ourselves practicing new numbers as we drove along in the car. On one such occasion, we were deeply engrossed in the song we were trying to perfect. Suddenly, we heard a third part coming from the back seat. We stopped singing and looked at each other in astonishment. It was our boy! How had we missed this? When asked about that, Chris stated matter-of-factly, "Oh, I always hear a third part when you guys sing." From that day forward, our duo became a trio.

With such natural musical ability, he excelled at every instrument he touched as well. What a joy it was to watch our miracle boy blossom in his faith as he used his gifts in such a powerful way!

I often marvel at the lengths the Lord will go to bless us and use us for His glory. Despite the way I had abused my body, He set me on an unexpected path so that I would be ready for the next leg of my journey with Him.

Since then, I've become acutely aware of my struggle with self-control. I still tend to slip into the notion that if a little bit of something is good, then a lot is a whole lot better. As a result, I've overexercised to the point of injury, suffered hair loss from lack of protein in my drastic diets, and been plagued with flat feet from spending too much time without the support of shoes. With each consequence came the reminder that I still have a ways to go in this area. I must say, however, that these episodes are coming with far less frequency. I am finally starting to learn that if I'm ever going to have victory in this area, knowing I *can* is not nearly as important as deciding I *won't*. I am so very thankful God never gives up on us. Aren't you?

Time to Reflect

"I would love to stop _____, but …"

Haven't we all been there—longing for the day when we won't be tempted beyond what we perceive as our limits? My friend, the simple truth is that God always provides a way out. At times, we are so distracted that we don't see the answer right in front of us. But most often, we're just not willing to wait for it. We fall into the same old pattern of behavior and then beat ourselves up for not being able to resist that temptation … again.

But I have some wonderful news for you! God's not finished with you yet! He sees your struggle, and He wants to see you living in victory, dear one.

In this exercise, you will dive into the deep—coming face-to-face with the very things that have been holding you captive for far too long.

First, let's take a few moments to set the stage. Grab a pen and paper, find yourself a comfortable spot, and light a candle or diffuse your favorite essential oil if you'd like. Have some soft, soothing music playing in the background. Close your eyes and invite the sweet presence of the Holy Spirit to fill you.

When you are ready, take some time to list the

things in your life that tend to challenge your sense of self-control. If you are someone with an addictive personality, this will be an easy task. Your temptations are fairly obvious, aren't they? But some of you may not even recognize the subtle seductions that lead you to sin. You don't even see them as sins. Rest assured, my friend, God thinks quite differently.

Read the following words found in the book of Proverbs 6:16–19.

Here are six things God hates, and one more that he loathes with a passion:

Eyes that are arrogant,
a tongue that lies,
hands that murder the innocent
a heart that hatches evil plots,
feet that race down a wicked track,
a mouth that lies under oath,
a troublemaker in the family. (MSG)

Now reread that passage, asking God to reveal the things in your life that displease Him that you're not aware of. The answers may not be easy to hear, but they are the most important words you could receive right now. Be honest with yourself. This is between you and God. Is there anything you need to add to your list?

Facing the truth about ourselves can be very

painful, can't it? But there is one more part to this cleansing process. Proverbs 28:13 says, "People who conceal their sins will not prosper, but if they confess and turn from them, they will receive mercy" (NLT). You have admitted your wrongdoing before Almighty God, but you must turn from those things to receive His mercy. My friend, that's repentance, and nothing pleases the Lord more. Come before Him now, just as you are. Call on the Holy Spirit and allow Him to heal your hurting soul.

Dear God, You know me better than I know myself. You and only You know the number of times You've lifted me back up after I've fallen to temptation. I am so tired of this pattern. Your Word tells me You were tempted in every way, just as we are—yet You never sinned (Heb. 4:15 NIV). I long to be more like You, Lord. Please forgive me and help me in my quest to conquer these things that control me. I know I can't do this alone. But You promised that You would not let me be tempted beyond what I can bear; that You would provide a way out so that I can endure it (1 Cor 10:13 NIV). Thank You for not abandoning me to my mistakes, for loving me too much to leave me where

I'm at. In this moment, I place my trust in You, my Lord and my God.

Prove by the way you live that you have repented of your sins and turned to God.
—Matthew 3:8 NLT

His Love for You

If you confess with your mouth Jesus as Lord
and believe in your heart that God raised
Him from the dead, you will be saved.
—Romans 10:9 NASB

Dear friends,

God has an amazing plan and purpose for your life,
and it begins with a decision—the most important
decision you will ever make. More than two thousand
years ago, Jesus, the one and only Son of God, hung on
a cross, taking the sin of the entire world on His body.
Your sin. Why would He do that? For one reason. Out
of His great love for you. What a precious gift! All you
need to do is accept it. If you would like to receive Him
as your Lord and your Savior and be assured of eternal
life with Him, please pray with me:

Dear God,

*I believe with all my heart that You gave Your one and
only Son for me, out of love, so that I would never have*

to be separated from You. I believe He rose from the dead, just as the Bible says.

I realize I'm a sinner and I have sinned against You. I am so very sorry for the things I have done. Please forgive me, God. I desperately need You. Right here and now, I turn from my sin and accept Jesus as my Lord and Savior. Please come into my heart and fill me with Your Holy Spirit. Help me become the person You created me to be. This I ask in Jesus's precious name. Amen.